Lessons Learned in the Janitorial Industry

The Lessons Learned Building a $19M Cleaning Company

Jordan Tong
Consultant, Elite BSC
CEO, Frantz Building Services

ISBN 978-1-7373320-3-9

Published 2021 by 315 Press
319 E 2nd Street
Owensboro, Kentucky, United States

Printed in the USA

Cover Design
By
Decree Design

Contents

Introduction

In 2005, I was a freshly minted Civil Engineering graduate from Tennessee Tech University. After taking a job in Nashville for a construction and site development firm, I was ready to take on the world. Nashville was buzzing with growth, music, entrepreneurship, and young talent ready to make a difference in the world. I loved this scene and was ready to take part in the action. However, in 2007, my wife and I made a trip back to our hometown of Owensboro, KY, to visit with family. While chatting with my dad he asked me a question that would ultimately change the course of my life. "Jordan, what would you think about moving back home and joining the family cleaning business?"

I knew nothing about running a business, much less a small cleaning business. But entrepreneurship was coursing through my veins. I'm a risk taker and leader by nature, and the idea of blazing a trail in the business world was enough to convince me to seize the opportunity.

To the outside world, this move probably looked a bit crazy. I had spent nearly five years getting a college degree (Yes, I was on the five year plan), and I was going to throw away this education to run a small cleaning business in western Kentucky. Why give up a promising career in one of the fastest growing cities in America to take over a third generation cleaning company? Working for the family cleaning business provided zero guarantee of pay raises, career advancement, or a secure retirement. But it did provide one thing I was hungry for: opportunity.

In the summer of 2007, my new job started at Frantz Building Services, our $1.5 million cleaning company. The first few months were spent managing some recently acquired new customers, assisting the sales rep on site visits, and occasionally cleaning at night. For over twenty years, the company had been doing business in one town, but the year I joined my dad began to make a push to grow the company into some new geographies within an hour of our base operation. This new growth would end up requiring me to work some late nights with the cleaning team and deal with early morning complaints from customers. I'll be honest, those were some long days!

Slowly but surely our company began to pick up some steam. Within a year, we were ready to officially separate the business in the new geography and create our first official branch location. This was followed by hiring a branch manager to run what had now grown to over $1,000,000 in revenue. Over the next five years, the company grew by an average of $600k in new revenue each year. We picked up new accounts in some surrounding areas and even started a new branch in Nashville, TN. After I took over running the day-to-day operations of the business, we began to add some additional key personnel.

Our first key hire was a new regional manager for the northern part of our operations. Then we brought on an HR generalist, then a new sales rep. We ironed out our financial statements and started setting goals, tracking expenses closely, and holding the branch managers accountable. The company not only was growing steadily, but our ability to execute effectively was improving. In 2019, we completed our first acquisition, and as of the time of this writing, our company is doing nearly $19 million in annual revenue.

If you are reading this short bio of our company, you might be tempted to think we followed a predictable path to success with few bumps in the road. But I can assure you this is not the case. During these years of growth, we failed over and over again. Stress levels were high at times. Failure sometimes seemed more likely than success. There were times when I felt alone, unsure, and wondered if we were doing things right. Don't get me wrong, by God's grace, we have found success and seen our company flourish. Many lives have been changed, careers built, and communities changed. But it was not an easy road.

The book you are about to read is a collection of thoughts, stories, and advice gathered over the last fourteen years. It is my hope that you can learn from my mistakes, laugh at my experiences, and profit from the knowledge we have learned over the years. We certainly don't have the market cornered on success in the janitorial industry, but what we have experienced is offered to you here.

Stories from the Trenches

1

Knife to My Throat

It was a normal day at my cleaning company. We held a sales strategy meeting, discussed a new account startup, worked on some recruiting strategies, and planned for the rest of the week. As the day was about to wrap up, I was handed an unemployment appeal written by a former employee (let's call him Dave). In this appeal was nearly a page describing how I had threatened this employee by holding a knife to his neck. (No, I'm not joking!) As I was reading the words on the page, I figured one of three things was happening: I was crazy, he was crazy, or this was just a dream from which I was about to wake.

This former employee worked at our company for about a year managing a large account. It was a tough job and he did a great job leading the team. However, the customer had a strong union and they petitioned to bring the work back in-house. Therefore, we lost the account. We didn't have another job to move Dave to, but we wanted to keep him on the team, partly out of loyalty to him and partly in hopes of using him at another project managed account in the near future.

We moved Dave into our office and let him help make cold calls with our sales team. However, we made it clear this was just a temporary job in the hopes of another account management role opening up. When it became evident that no local management spot was going to come available, we told Dave he had about sixty days to find another job. We gave him freedom to job hunt during his time with us and even gave him thirty days of severance pay. All of this was done in hopes of Dave finding another job before ending employment with us. In fact, we even approached one of our existing customers to help Dave get an interview, going so far as to write several reference letters for him.

Despite this effort on our part, he seemed in no rush to get a job, then slandered our company in his unemployment claim. And yes, this included the outlandish accusation against me. I'm not sure the purpose of the accusation, but he went into graphic detail about how I held a five-inch knife to his carotid artery and kept it there for approximately five seconds. I'm still confused and frequently laugh at the situation, but such is life as a business owner in the cleaning industry. And just to clarify, I did not put a knife up to his throat, in case you were wondering.

So what did I learn through this experience? First, sometimes when you do the right thing, people will still treat you unfairly. However, this is never an excuse to not do the right thing. Jesus, the only man who did no wrong, was falsely accused and killed, yet this did not cause him to retaliate or waver in his course. Likewise, we should always do the morally right thing as business owners. Second, even when trying to do the right thing, we must use wisdom and good common sense. In a case such as this, I should have given Dave two options: take severance and submit a resignation or terminate and agree to let him draw unemployment. Instead, I basically gave him severance in faith that he would not be the type of person who would want to draw unemployment.

We won the unemployment claim. I no longer carry a knife.

2

Letter from a Cleaner I Never Met

This morning I received an email with the subject line, "Final Week." My mind instantly jumped to two possible scenarios, both negative. Did we just lose a key manager? Did a customer terminate our agreement? Much to my delight, it was neither. In fact, it was something I was not expecting from a cleaner I had never met working at a jobsite I've never visited. After reading what Patrick wrote, I could not be more proud of my company.

More than ever, I am convinced that building a unique and impactful company culture is the primary job of leadership. Everything flows from here. This is especially true in the janitorial industry, where most of our team members work remotely and rarely have contact with corporate leadership. However, the task has always seemed so daunting. How can I foster a unique "feel" throughout the organization when we have 500 people spread across four states? Well, don't be dismayed, because it can be done, and it starts with a conviction and clear vision of what your organization should look like.

At Frantz Building Services, we want a culture that embodies three things:

- Passionately and with excellence serve others (customers and each other)
- Genuinely care for people
- Do everything with the utmost integrity

We talk about this in our meetings. We write about it in our newsletters. We teach on it at training sessions. We screen for it during interviews. We are committed to living it out.

Do we fail? You bet! Could we do better? Yes! Do we have a long way to go? Absolutely! But when we get letters like this from Patrick, who works at a dirty, nasty factory, it gives hope that change is happening. We must keep pressing on and fighting the good fight of positively shaping our company culture. Be encouraged! Your hard work will pay off. Your people and your customers will be better off. And your company will thrive.

Enjoy these heartfelt words from a cleaning team member, and remember that your leadership matters.

"This week is going to be my final week working for Frantz. This company has shown me a lot and taught me a lot about being a family with all of you. This company has been the best place to work I ever had the privilege to work for. No company will ever be able to show the support and love that everyone here has for me. I have met a lot of

different people working here and all of you have been so nice and helpful with any questions I have had. I truly regret having to leave this company and all of you, but its what's best for my family and the new baby (on way lol). When my baby gets born and older I will tell her about the best place I ever worked and she should strive to work for a company just like this one. With all of you working here this company will grow and become one of the biggest and strongest companies around the U.S. I will truly miss all of you. God bless all of you and I hope everything goes well for this company."

3

Losing My Largest Account

We all dread that phone call from one of our large customers. You know the one. "We are sorry, but as of today, you're on your official 30-day notice of termination." While the feelings of panic were much greater during the early stages of our business, that call still stings. Lost business is rarely a good thing. Perhaps you picked the wrong customer, your service is bad, the economy is weakening, or a corporate mandate required them to accept the low bid. Our natural reaction is to justify the loss to remove the sting of rejection. However, even the losses that are "out of your hands" come with a level of responsibility you must shoulder and learn from. This is one such loss.

2017 was a record sales and profit year for our company. While growth can be a great boost to a company, it can become a strain if it all happens at once. That is exactly what happened to us. Over the course of the year, we grew from about $15k/month to $145k/month in one particular city.

Because of this rapid growth, we needed a branch office, area and project managers, a branch manager, and startup teams to kick off the 4-5 new accounts in the area. One of our managers was transferred from another branch; however, the rest of the local operation was built from scratch.

During the 3rd quarter of 2017, we landed an account unlike anything we had serviced in the past. This facility ran nearly 24/7, 365 days per year and was staffed with a 10anitorrial team around the clock. Before we took over the account, they were servicing the entire facility using their own in-house team. While we petitioned for the entire project, they decided to give us the 3rd shift portion of the program, the most difficult piece of the pie.

While the contract was nearly $20k/month, it presented us with many challenges. First, our 3rd shift workers were making less than the 1st and 2nd shift in-house staff, creating a recruiting challenge for us in this rural location. Second, partnering with the in-house staff and reporting to a daytime janitorial manager created a tension that seemed unresolvable. Finally, a strictly 3rd shift crew created some recruiting and retention problems for us.

Lessons Learned

At the end of the day, we just were not able to satisfy our client. There are a few reasons why I believe this to be the case; however, we plan to learn from these lessons and go forward stronger.

Too much too fast

If this nearly $2,000,000 in business had been spread out across multiple branch locations, keeping a more consistent operation would have been much easier. Going forward, we will be leery of accepting too much business in one concentrated area. We would rather serve fewer customers well than more customers poorly.

Don't take the leftovers

We should not have accepted an account that forced us to do what the customer wasn't willing to do for less than the customer was originally paying.

Don't partner with in-house staff

When in-house staff and outsourced providers partner on a project, there is always room for much tension and gossip. If at all possible, avoid situations where the in-house staff has a motive to disparage your company.

3rd shift only is tough

When you have a large account that is comprised of 1st, 2nd and 3rd shifts, multiple layers of resources can be drawn upon. Additionally, shifts can cover for one another and balance each other out. When you only have 3rd shift, this can create some difficulties.

Taken as a whole, the above reasons caused us to lose the account. I'm sure I've left out others. Nonetheless, we hope to learn from this experience, improve our processes, and show ourselves stronger in years to come.

*This article was originally written in 2018. In 2020, we won back this customer that we had lost.

4

Ghost Employees

When I first heard the ghost employee story, it sent me scrambling back to my business to see if I was protected. My friend - lets call him John - had lost nearly $1,000,000 over the course of ten years through employee embezzlement and he honestly didn't ever know it was happening. John is a smart businessman, had built a large BSC, and had multiple controls in place to ensure fiscal responsibility throughout the organization. However, there were a few loopholes that some corrupt individuals took advantage of for many years. Here's what happened.

A dishonest manager at a branch location was responsible for hiring his employees, getting their paperwork filled out, turning in and/or approving their hours, and delivering their paycheck. Once he realized that no checks and balances were in place to prevent ghost employee fraud, he created ghost employees using fraudulent IDs, I-9 information, and contact information. To make these employees fly under the radar, the crooked manager found a few jobs that were running under budget and put the ghost employees on these accounts. Therefore, the accounts stayed under budget and no corporate eyebrows were raised.

When it came time to pay the ghost employees, the paychecks were sent to the corrupt manager (to be delivered to the employees), who then cashed those ghost checks at a less-than-reputable check-cashing outfit. Even after the company switched to mainly automated timekeeping systems and direct deposit, some employees weren't required to use the clock-in systems and some used pay cards as opposed to direct deposit. One larger account was making the crooked manager nearly $2,000 per month for nearly TEN YEARS!!

So what can you learn from this story? How can you prevent something like this from happening at your company? How can you implement reasonable safeguards without creating a dictatorship?

First, do background checks and use E-verify to help ensure applicants are in fact real persons eligible to work in the US and living in the area of the job. Second, have someone at the main office call and personally speak with each new employee. This is a good way to ensure corporate is engaged with every employee, boosting morale in the process.

Third, require every employee to use direct deposit and submit a voided check. Fourth, force all employees to clock in using a digital timekeeping system, preferably one that is caller-ID tracked or done with a geofence. Fifth, monitor your jobsite hours each and every day. John's company was doing this, but still had issues. Nevertheless, it is one additional check on the system. Finally, on large jobs, consider using a biometric scanner.

Employee theft is nothing new because human hearts haven't changed. Boundaries are good for us all because desire can overcome reason and morals. Be it company time, illegitimate tax deductions, or another's spouse, thievery is no respecter of persons. A competent leader is aware of these proclivities and erects appropriate safeguards to prevent unnecessary temptation. Call it love, protection, or self-preservation, checks and balances are just good business.

5

Failed Business Venture

A few years ago, our janitorial company created a totally separate division we were sure was going to make money. The cleaning company was doing well financially, I now had some free time on my hands, and I wanted to add value by creating a new revenue stream for the company. It was a total failure! While we did make money the first year, we lost money in the second and the stress level was more that I wanted. Making matters worse, this new venture detracted us from the core janitorial business, which was a big mistake. Let me explain what happened.

My company, Frantz Building Services, is co-owned by my parents and me. In 2015, the company was going strong and our leadership team was solid. In fact, the leadership team was so solid that the company was running very smoothly with little effort required on my part. Being the entrepreneurial-minded person I am, I decided a new business venture would be a good way to spend my time. My dad grew up in the construction industry and was a very skilled carpenter. My college degree was in Civil Engineering and I had experience in estimating and managing large construction projects. So in my mind, creating a construction division was an obvious choice.

To justify my decision, I assumed we could use this service to add value to our existing clients. Why not offer them construction services in addition to janitorial? It seemed so obvious. We had the skill set, the finances, and the time to do it. So why not?

While getting work for existing clients was my goal, it quickly became apparent that in our smaller city residential work was going to be the only way we could get this new division off the ground. So with a minimum job size in mind, we took off selling and picking up new clients. I was excited and getting jobs was not a problem. During our first fiscal year, we did nearly $750,000 in revenue. However, as we began to grow, challenges began to surface and life got stressful. The grind to pick up new business was constant, wrangling subs to get work done was exhausting, and keeping good workers was challenging.

Of course, this is nothing new to the construction industry, but what I didn't foresee was how much this new venture pulled me away from my janitorial business. What began as a mission to add value to our company turned into an all-consuming venture that detached me from the very thing that made the new division possible.

The construction division did not add value to our janitorial business, and if anything, it diluted what we had, as it pulled key leaders away from our bread and butter. As stress mounted and profits eroded in year two, we realized the mistake we had made. Our focused drifted and we did not give our core business the attention it deserved. I'm not sure there were any immediate consequences to the janitorial business, but one thing is sure. I wasted time away from the business that could have been used pouring into our people. The grass looked greener and I fell for the allure of something new.

Lessons Learned

So, what can you learn from my mistake? Not all new business ventures or add-on divisions are a bad idea. But before you dive off into a new venture, ask yourself these key questions.

Will this new division truly add value to my core customers? Is it a service they value and would pay a premium for me to provide?

Does this new division add to or subtract from my perceived value? If you perform poorly in the new division, this could ruin the image of your current core business.

Does this new venture create synergies with my core business? For instance, adding a carpet cleaning crew certainly adds synergy and can easily tuck into a janitorial operation. However, a construction division like mine did not create such synergies. If synergies are not realized, the new venture is not a division but rather akin to starting a brand new company in a brand new industry.

Is your time best spent pouring into your existing business, cultivating for future success? Or is you time best spend outside the business?

My intention is not to scare or deter you from trying new things, but to warn you that shiny stuff syndrome has damaged many, many businesses. Don't invest in other fields while your own is being taken over by weeds.

Strategy

6

What Strategy Is and Is Not

You want to grow your company. You want to be a better company, maybe the best. You want to stand out from your competition. So, what do you do? You develop what you think is a strategy. You find ways to cut costs, be more efficient, and maybe sell more products or services to your customers. Better, cheaper, faster. This is the key to setting yourself apart…or so you thought!

When companies consider how to grow their revenue, profit, and market share, they often think in terms of making their operation more efficient. This, they think, is their strategy. While such efficiencies may help improve profits and growth in the short run, it will not produce long term benefits for the company. The reason is that every company is pursuing these same things. And if everyone is getting better, faster, cheaper, then comparatively, everyone is still the same. And what's more, as you get increasingly efficient, the harder it becomes to make additional efficiency gains. The law of diminishing returns places a significant restraint on this so-called strategy. So let me repeat, "operational efficiency is *not* strategy."

So how is strategy different from operational effectiveness? Strategy is carving out a niche for yourself in the marketplace – a way to differentiate your company from others. Operational effectiveness is making yourself better or faster, regardless of niche. Strategy is a way to provide greater value to your customers at a similar price, or similar value at a lower price. Operational effectiveness, on the other hand, is just making your company run more smoothly. This may have short-term benefits, but in the long run, you will be no different than your competitors, as these things are easily replicable, thus giving no advantage to anyone. A company can only become so productive before quality drops.

Now this does not mean operational effectiveness is unimportant. Competitors will be striving for operational effectiveness and if we choose to neglect this aspect, we will either lose customers or see profit margins dwindle. But operational efficiency alone will not truly differentiate you from your competitors. Even worse, it will not make you more profitable in the long run. As Michael Porter says in his Harvard Business Review article, *What is Strategy*, "Constant improvement in operational effectiveness is necessary to achieve superior profitability. However, it is not usually sufficient. Few companies have competed successfully on the basis of operational effectiveness over an extended period, and staying ahead of rivals gets harder every day." If your company has no real strategy and competes only on the basis of operational effectiveness, then you have become a commodity, no different than buying gas from Shell or Chevron.

The challenge for every cleaning contractor is finding a way to truly differentiate your company in the marketplace. Increasing your production rate to 5,000sf/hr is not a sufficient answer.

7

Barriers to Scaling Up

Scaling up your janitorial company is a motivation most owners in the industry have. The benefits to customers, employees, and the company are endless. But despite our desire, very few companies make it to a place where the company is on a long-term growth trajectory. If the foundation for scaling is not in place, growth may happen, but it won't be sustainable.

Considering this, there are three barriers to scaling up. If you overcome these barriers, growth becomes a thrill and an asset to the organization. Failure to overcome these barriers makes growth an anchor dragging your company down. According to Verne Harnish, author of *Scaling Up*, there are three impediments to scaling up your organization. These barriers are as follows:

Leadership: the inability to staff/grow enough leaders throughout the organization who have capabilities to delegate and predict.

Scalable infrastructure: the lack of systems and structures (physical and organizational) to handle the complexities in communication and decisions coming with growth.

Marketing: the failure to scale up an effective marketing function to both attract new relationships (customers, talent, etc.) to the business and address the increased competitive pressures (and eroding margins) as you scale.

As a company grows, so does complexity. During the early stages of every business, the owner can handle key relationships, ensure financial stability and controls, interview and hire as needed, connect with each employee, ensure quality, etc. But with each stage of growth, complexity mounts exponentially. Using the example of communication channels, with two people there are two channels of communication. With three people there are six channels, and with four people there are twelve channels of communication. As you grow, complexity mounts and makes the job of owner-operator much harder. With less than 0.4% of all companies reaching $10,000,000 in revenue, we can see how these barriers are rarely tackled.

So how can leadership, a scalable infrastructure, and marketing help overcome the complexity challenge? Let's take each in turn.

Elite leadership overcomes the complexity challenge by carrying out the company strategy through effective delegation and management. These leaders become business owners within the business, "owning" and integrating a certain piece of the whole. They understand and value the culture, purpose, and values and infuse their team and operation with those things. These men and women are not mere managers working within set standard operating procedures, but influencers of people, driving them to accomplish the goals set before them.

Scalable infrastructures are the road we lay upon which our leadership and their teams will travel. They are the ways we do business that allow us to move from ten customers to one hundred or one thousand. For instance, if you have a method of delivering your service that would not work in another city or with 10x the clients you currently have, then you are setting your company up to hit an inevitable wall. Just as the systems of the human body are designed to grow from a single cell in utero to a full-grown adult, so too must a company's systems be ready for growth.

Finally, and perhaps surprisingly, marketing is key to "getting it right" in the long run. To quote Harnish: "To prevent margin erosion, marketing's role (with lots of customer input) is to determine the right "what" we should be selling to the best "whos"; and how best we should sell at the right price...if not, sales teams will chase any low hanging fruit they can find which is the quickest way to defocus the business and crush your margins."

As a business owner, your job is to see these barriers and make steps to overcome them. Regardless of the growth phase you are in, I recommend the following as first steps to moving in the right direction:

Leadership: Identify the next critical, key leadership position in your company and create a position profile for it. Define exactly what you are looking for and begin looking "just before" you think you can afford it.

Scalable Infrastructure: Over the next sixty days, create a scalable process for each of the key functions of your organization (i.e. HR, finance, sales, and operations).

Marketing: Define your ideal client, identify their deepest needs, and develop a plan to target those prospects.

8

Four Keys to an Annual Business Plan

Hope is the fuel of the human soul, the promise of a better future. Not only do we need hope as individuals, but our businesses need it as well. Our team needs a goal to rally around, a challenge of making next year better than the last. But in order to make your next year a better one in your BSC, you need a plan. You need goals to achieve and a path to hit those goals. As you and your team prepare for the coming year, here are four areas a plan in necessary.

Culture

Company culture is the identity and moral fabric of the company. If you aren't intentional about your culture, it will create itself. And this is not always a good thing. First, find ways for you and your team to emphasize culture. A company newsletter, leadership time in the field, orientation, and host of other methods can be employed to push the cultural message. Remember, people may join your company for the pay and opportunity, but they stay because of culture.

People

Every new business plan should have some plan to develop people. Future success depends on future leaders. At a bare minimum, you need succession plans in place for key positions and a training program for managers and supervisors. If you don't have a training program, shoot me an email and I can point you in the right direction.

Sales

If you aren't growing, you are likely dying as a company. So not only do you need new sales goals for next year, but you need micro-goals to ensure you hit the big picture goals. Let me challenge you to have a total sales goal, a proposals delivered goal, a phone calls per week goal, and an in-person meetings goal. Having an annual revenue goal doesn't help if you aren't hitting the smaller goals throughout the year.

Operations

Finally, you need operations goals and plans for the coming year. I would recommend a few things:

- Select several accounts that you want to reduce labor on
- Identify pieces of equipment you want to replace or upgrade
- Create a plan to increase applications and reduce employee turnover

- Identify contracts that need to be renegotiated and renewed
- Identify customers that need price increases

If you can put together a small plan and execute in the upcoming year, you will have a better year. This will not only increase the bottom line, but it will create excitement and energy in your BSC. Remember, if you fail to plan, you plan to fail.

9

Why We Fired Half Our Customers in One Year

The number one goal of most small companies is to increase revenue. We have a hump to get over, we want to grow, and we want to build a great business. How do we do this? We try to get more clients and serve them well. However, what if I told you that the best thing you can do to grow your business is to fire some of your existing customers? What?!? Yes, and this is exactly what we did recently at one of our branch locations. In fact, we fired nearly half of our customers in an effort to strengthen our local operation. Let me share some of the details.

The Background

One of our branch operations, our smallest branch at the time, was comprised of two very large accounts and a handful of small and medium sized accounts. These accounts were spread out over a 30-mile radius. Our management team was comprised of two project managers (managing the two large accounts), one branch manager, and an area manager (who managed the small/medium sized accounts). Of the accounts the area manager handled, three of them were pretty self-sufficient. The other seven accounts were comprised of about 20 buildings and required pretty intense management effort. The total revenue managed by the Area Manager was about $500k/yr. We had some trouble staffing the Area Manager job, making it the highest turnover management position in the company.

The Problem Identified

The definition of insanity is to do the same thing over and over again while expecting a different result. That is what we were doing. In fact, things got so stressful at one point that our Sr. Management team was coming in from out of town to help with all aspects of the local operation, and our local branch manager ended up in the hospital with stress induced anxiety and chest pains. Yea, things were bad.

After allowing this chaos to persist for several months, we sat down and began to analyze our operation, and specifically the accounts that were causing us the most trouble. Some of the headache was due to demanding small clients, some was attributed to difficult accounts to staff, and still other headaches were coming from accounts that had multiple buildings spread over a large geography. We then took the 6 most troublesome accounts (totaling 15+ buildings), totaled up the profit generated from those accounts, and quickly realized it was equal to what we were paying our Area Manager.

The Solution Implemented

Because our Area Manager was looking to make a career transition, we decided to fire all six of those clients and completely eliminate that area manager position. Doing so eliminated our most troublesome and least profitable accounts, eliminated a management position, and caused our profit to drop by zero dollars! Our branch manager now manages the four remaining accounts, while the project managers continue to manage their single-site large customers. In essence, we streamlined our operations, eliminated headache and stress, and removed unprofitable business. We are now more profitable with less business, something I never thought I'd say.

To be fair, you do increase risk by reducing your customer base. However, we now have a renewed focus on getting the right kinds of clients going forward – clients that are easier to manage, staff, and profit from.

The Lesson Learned

Anytime you make a mistake, you should always look back and learn from those mistakes. Mistakes are only beneficial when you make changes to prevent them from happening again. The key lesson we learned was this: *only pursue the right types of accounts. Not all revenue is good revenue!*

I would encourage you to do the same. Figure out what types of customers ideally suit your business model then relentlessly pursue them. Additionally, know when to say "no" to the wrong kinds of business. Chaos and managers in the hospital is a lesson you need not experience. Learn from me and don't make the mistakes we have made. Trust me, your team will thank you for it.

10

Why Small Businesses Fail to Grow

According to the U.S. Bureau of Labor Statistics, 50% of all businesses fail within the first five years and 66% fail within the first 10 years. But perhaps worse than that, of those that do survive, most fail to really thrive. Most fail to scale up, have consistently excellent revenue growth, beat industry average profit margins, and give the owner more freedom. Most business owners feel that the company owns them instead of them owning the company. Why does this happen? Better yet, why does that almost always happen?

Certainly, you have talked to business owners with this story. Here are common refrains. "We are just getting by." "It's tough out there - a real jungle." "It's hard to get good people. If I could only get good people." "One of these days I'll get some freedom from this place."

These are not the comments of the owner of a thriving business. These are the comments of someone who has bought a job, and it owns them! But I promise you, there is a better way - a proven path that successful businesses have taken.

As I survey small businesses, I see one common thread amongst those who struggle to thrive, and a different commonality among those who thrive. While there are many steps necessary to building a great company (e.g. impactful culture, strategy, healthy leadership, etc.), there is one core principle that must be grasped above all else. And here it is:

Instead of working "in the business", the owner must create a scalable operation by working "on the business."

Now I know what you are thinking. This is old news - work on my business not in my business. Well, yes and no. It is old news in the sense that this adage has been around for some time. But don't let its age fool you into thinking it is outdated. However, this principle is new in that the focus of the owner is on creating a "scalable operation." So let's break this down into three stages using a fictional story.

Stage 1 - Working in the business (The E-myth)

Jeff has been working as a project manager for a large construction company. He put together estimates, helped sell projects, and oversaw the construction process. Driven by dreams of personal and financial freedom, he steps out to start his own construction company. He knows the business and thinks he can create a successful company. He sets to work doing what he knows best, bidding work and managing it. On top of that, he must handle the finances, administration, and everything else needed to keep the doors open. Jeff, however, has fallen prey to what Michael Gerber famously described as the E-Myth. Jeff thinks his success as a project manager will translate to success in running his new business. However, despite being in the construction industry (an industry he knows well), the skills needed to succeed as a project manager are different than the skills needed to run a successful company. As the adage goes, "what got you here won't get you there."

Jeff has bought a job, and at times he wonders why in the world he went out on his own. Not only is he now working longer hours, but he feels the full weight of the stress of owning and running the business. For Jeff to gain a sense of freedom and for the business to have the chance of truly succeeding, Jeff must move to stage 2, working on the business. The business must take on a life of its own.

Stage 2 - Working on the business (The Real Business Owner)
For the business to produce more beyond the result of Jeff's direct efforts, it must begin to take on a life of its own. What does this mean? The business must be set up such that it begins to operate without the direct effort of its owner. The cliche phrase often used for this concept is working on the business, not in the business. Systems and processes must be put in place that give employees direction. You are not creating robots but creating a framework within which your team members will operate. They have freedom within boundaries, aimed at certain objectives.

To use an example, Jeff may develop a system for handling the human resources and administrative functions of the business. Hiring and onboarding is done in a very specific way. Phone calls are answered with consistency. Inventory is tracked in a specific way at regularly defined intervals. Jeff then hires an individual to carry out this clearly defined process. This portion of the company soon begins to run smoothly without the regular and direct involvement of Jeff. A system has been designed and a competent individual is owning and managing that system. Jeff then creates a similar system for the financial aspect of the business, then project management, sales, etc. Just like the systems of a car must all function properly for the car to run without the owner pushing it, so too must the various functions of the business operate independently yet aimed toward a common goal.

Stage 3 - Creating a scalable operation (The True CEO)

Most people see a successful implementation of stage 2 to be a great success. And to be fair, it is a great achievement. Few businesses get this far. But most entrepreneurs are not satisfied with this level of success. The motivation goes beyond a sustainable business – they want a great business that can perpetually grow, create more freedom, more jobs, more money, and more impact. To put it shortly, they want to scale up! This is tangentially related to Jim Collin's famous concept of going from Good to Great. Just as going from Stage 1 to Stage 2 takes a certain mindset, going from Stage 2 to Stage 3 (the scaling up phase) takes a unique mindset and set of actions from the owner. So, what does this look like?

In Stage 2, the focus was on creating standard systems that people could carry out, slowly freeing the owner from "handling" every aspect of the business. Stage three imagines what a scaled-up company would look like, then focuses on the critical areas that will make this vision a success. These include:

- Specific company culture built around a core purpose and set of values.
- Strategy that guides the growth and operational decisions of the business.
- Scalable infrastructure (i.e. the standard processes are designed to be scalable)
- Dedication to hiring high level leaders combined with position profiles and compensation plans to inspire growth and company success.
- A plan for financial controls that places the health of the company over other priorities.

To go back to our example, Jeff must communicate the culture of the firm and ensure that it is known, believed, and not lost during growth. He must develop or refine the strategy of the company to ensure the long-term focus of the company does not suffer at the expense of the allure of growth. A dedication to a certain service offering made them successful, and this hard-core focus is the only thing that will ensure success in the long run. Chasing growth for growth's sake is certain to dilute the value of Jeff's company and doom them to mediocrity at best, failure at worst.

Jeff must also plan for operational systems and procedures that allow his company to operate successfully in any geography they desire to work in. They need systems that will scale from $1M to $20M, 1 office to 5. Fourth, he must swallow his pride and hire leaders who are the best, dare I say better than Jeff himself. A great leader must be humble enough to realize he needs men and women more talented than himself to scale up the business. Finally, Jeff must develop financial controls that are radically aimed at the long-term health of the business. Better cash flow, less risk, and well-compensated (thriving) employees are key to growth and sustained success.

11

Strategy Is Not What You Think

In the world of business, few terms get thrown around more often than the word "strategy." And trust me, the janitorial industry is no exception. But oddly enough, despite the frequent talk of strategy, few people understand what strategy really is. We know strategy is important and that we should have one, but our "strategy talk" is quickly reduced to how we can increase our operational or sales effectiveness. But effectiveness and efficiency are not strategy - not in the janitorial industry or any industry. As Sun Tzu said, "Tactics without strategy is the noise before defeat."

Strategy is complicated, yet staggeringly simple. In its essence, strategy is about making choices. There are three simple questions you must answer when formulating your company strategy.

- What will you do as a company?
- What will you not do?

- How will you create advantage over the competition?

Now don't be fooled by the simplicity of these questions. They are more profound than you can imagine and not easily answered. Let's break them down, one by one.

What will you do as a company?

Most janitorial companies fail not from a lack of opportunities, but from not choosing the right opportunities. Any entrepreneur will soon realize that money can be made in an infinite number of ways. But a strategic leader will pick the few opportunities to chase and build a business around those. In the janitorial industry, this is no different. Cleaning is an incredibly broad industry that could encompass a myriad of options. ServiceMaster focuses on schools, hospitals, and other large institutions. Sodexo has built a business on serving clients who have both facility and food service needs. Merry Maids sticks only to residential service. A friend of mine in Colorado has built his janitorial business servicing medical facilities.

Now all of these are very obvious instances of "what will you do." However, you too must answer the same question. To create market dominance and maintain long term success, you must pick your niche. Chasing every opportunity is a sure way to sink the ship, one leak at a time. Being a janitorial company that does everything for everybody is a sure way to be known and respected by nobody.

Here are a few questions to help you begin the journey of getting this first step right.

- What types of customers am I best suited to serve? Retail? Medical? Manufacturing? Residential? Local office? Corporate office? High rise? Public venue?
- What existing strengths do I have (or strengths I could develop) that position me well to serve a particular niche?
- Are there certain geographic markets I would thrive in? Big city vs. small city?
- Am I well positioned to service small customers or large customers?

Answering the "who will I serve" question will help you develop a plan to uniquely serve this client base in a way no other competitor can. You can't create a competitive advantage when everyone is your customer and every service is on your list of offerings.

Keep in mind that the above questions do not mean you must pick one type of customer or one location. However, there should be a combination of choices that creates a customer base that makes sense. For instance, at my company, we have chosen a few client types that are located in certain types of geographies. This allows us to focus on the key activities that help maintain a competitive advantage in our area of specialty.

What will you not do?

This question is equally important as question number one. In fact, Michael Porter of the Harvard Business School argues it is more important. He says, "The essence of strategy is choosing what NOT to do." By knowing what you will not do, you add a level of clarity to what you will do. By saying, "we will not service retail clients," you are indicating you are not well suited to take on 3rd shift, tenant leased clients where you don't have regular interaction with the decision maker. Some companies have found a way to thrive on retail, but others choose to stay away.

The most difficult part of saying "no" is actually following through on your commitment. Every compromise veers you off the strategic path, jeopardizing your strategic position. Going back to our retail example, if nearly all your clients are manufacturers who are cleaned on 2nd shift, a retail client would force you to recruit for and manage a 3rd shift job. Such tasks could potentially divert your management team from servicing primary customers. Your operation should have a "fit" across all activities, creating a synergy not easily diffused.

How will you create advantage over the competition?

This is what everyone wants to know: How can I stand above my competition? How can I position myself as the superior janitorial contractor in the markets I serve? What is it that will differentiate me from my peers in the industry?

While I wish I had a silver bullet for you, the plain truth is that differentiation in the janitorial industry is hard. In every mature industry, competitive advantage is difficult to achieve, but don't lose heart. Companies like Southwest, Chick-fil-A, and Honda have done it. You can too.

Let me conclude with an example of how a company could create a competitive advantage in the janitorial industry.

ABC Janitorial is located in a large metropolitan area filled with multi-tenant, property-managed buildings. ABC has seen the opportunity and created a business model that fits the needs of this client type, giving ABC an advantage over their competition. These property-managed buildings are primarily price driven, but have other unique needs. For instance, they constantly have tenants turning over, requiring spaces to be deep cleaned and prepped for new clients. Additionally, each building has multiple tenants which means multiple clients to know and keep happy. Finally, these clients often have diverse "handyman needs" which the property managers must find solutions to.

ABC janitorial has built its business around these unique needs of property management firms. They utilize cloud-based programs to manage the multiple client needs, relationships, and requests. This helps the property managers stay in tune with tenant needs. Additionally, they have specialty crews to help with tenant turnover cleanups, handyman services, and more. They have built a model of supervision that knows and understands multi-tenant space. ABC janitorial is strategically positioned to serve property management companies well and outperform their would-be competitors.

So, what will your strategy be? You can't beat industry averages in growth and profit over long periods of time without a sound strategy. Spend the time to be clear on this foundational issue.

12

Four Rules for a Family Business

Family businesses can be a blessing and a curse, sometimes both at the same time. We've all heard the horror stories of family businesses gone bad, and maybe you are in the midst of one of those horror stories. However, a family cleaning business can also be a source of tremendous blessing. So, what can you do to make your family business thrive? Let me offer four principles to keep your business free of strife, ill-will, and bad blood.

Keep work at work and home at home

Good family businesses know how to keep a good work-home balance. Parents and children who work together need to know how to operate as co-workers as well as in their familial relationships. Confusing the two will create unrest. When it's family time, then just be family. You don't need to be "the boss" at Thanksgiving dinner. Learn the boundaries, then stick to them.

Have clearly defined roles

Having clearly defined roles in your company is critical, especially for family members working in the company. Each family member needs to know their role and operate respectfully within that role. When expectations are not clearly defined, apathy can seep in. When worker apathy starts, bitterness and ill-will are soon to follow. The antidote to this is crystal clear roles and accountability.

No nepotism

Hiring family members can be a wonderful thing when everyone is performing well. However, when a family member is underperforming, other family members and outsider employees can become resentful. Therefore, family members *must* be held to the same performance standards as other employees. Favoritism not only hurts other employees, but the lagging family member as well. Not expecting the best out of a person is to condone sub-par work. This sets a person up for long-term failure.

Don't let money divide

Finally, and perhaps most importantly, don't let greed ruin family/work relationships. Your family is way more important than the extra $10,000 you could have made last year. If the first three rules are operating as they should, then generosity will only enhance the work-family relationship. But when the person in control is greedy or stingy, bitterness will almost always result. We've all heard the Bible verse that says, "the love of money is the root of all kinds of evil." A truer statement has never been uttered, especially when it comes to family business.

Practice these four principles and you will be on your way to cultivating a thriving family business.

13

When Is a Cleaning Account Too Small?

The natural inclination of most business owners and salespeople is to get new business at all costs. If it can grow the top line (and hopefully the bottom line), then it should be pursued. This tendency is common in the commercial cleaning industry as well. Companies often chase work outside monthly cleaning contracts, pulling their operations in many different directions. However, accounts too small can be equally damaging to your operation. *But how small is too small?*

Can you achieve a net profit?

The first question to answer is whether or not you can be profitable with a group of small accounts. And here I'm not referring to job profitability but profit after management and overhead expenses. Let's assume a full-time manager can oversee 30 small accounts. Assuming a $35k/yr salary plus vehicle, gas, benefits, etc., your direct "overhead" costs run about $4,200/month (not including company overhead).

Assuming your profit margin is 40% on small accounts, this means your average job size on 30 accounts needs to be nearly $400/month just to break even. So, with this simple example, you can see that some jobs truly are too small. If you are going to hire full time management, it is very difficult to be profitable with accounts less than $500/month. If you want to grow a company greater than $1M in revenue, your average account size must be north of $1,000/month.

The hidden costs of small accounts

In addition to low profit dollars, small accounts have a few other disadvantages. First, they usually entail minimal amounts of labor hours only a few times a week. These jobs can be difficult to staff unless paired with other accounts. Second, small accounts usually care a great deal about the money they spend on cleaning services. They are watching their expenses closely; therefore, you may catch more grief from a small customer than with a large one. Finally, managing small accounts takes away time and energy that could be spent servicing larger, more profitable accounts. This is known as opportunity cost. When you say "Yes" to one customer, you likely are saying "no" to another.

So, while small accounts may be necessary on the path to growth, you likely won't build a successful cleaning company with this model. Pay attention to the true costs of managing your customer to find out which client mix is right for you.

14

Three Ways to Branch Out

There are three main ways to branch out your cleaning company into a new geographic territory: large accounts, boot strapping, and acquisition. All three are viable options, each with their own strengths and weaknesses. In this article and the following two, I'm going to describe each method and then list the strengths and weaknesses of each. Depending upon your current situation, one method will likely be superior to the others. However, the goal of each is the same - start a new operation in a new geographic location.

Description: The Large Account Method

In this method of branching out, the goal is to create a new operation by securing a large contract in a new geographic location. By large account, I am referring to a customer that bills at least $15k/month and has an on-site manager built into the account. The idea behind this approach is that with one account, your company can have instant revenue combined with a capable manager who could potentially take on new growth.

Strengths of This Method

There are two obvious strengths of this method. The first is the minimal amount of capital investment needed to start a new branch location. If you can land a large account in a new city, the sales and startup costs are your only expenses. The second strength of this method is that you have a manager built into your new branch startup and he/she is being paid for by the new customer. Many large companies in the cleaning industry have grown this way, starting branch operations wherever they could find large customers.

Weaknesses of This Method

While this method of growth is preferred by many, there are some downsides. First, it could take a significant amount of time to find the sort of account that can house an on-site manager. Second, it can be very difficult to land a large account in an area that you don't have a presence in. Customers are often reluctant to give an account to an unproven, out-of-town contractor. In our experience, this has been the chief obstacle of growth by this method. However, if you can develop a specialty dealing with a certain type of customer, you can often overcome this objection.

Another way, similar to large account acquisition but a different strategy, is what I have dubbed "bootstrapping." Along with large account acquisition, this has been my company's preferred and most successful form of growing. While not for everyone, this method can be very effective if combined with the right long-term strategy. Additionally, it can have some positive impact on your selling process as well. So let's dive in and look at what this strategy is along with some positives and negatives associated with it.

Description: The Bootstrapping Method

The bootstrapping method of growth consists of the following: identifying a new territory you want to grow in, targeting all accounts that you would like to have, and committing whatever financial and management resources necessary to make the new branch succeed. Instead of waiting for a large account to "anchor" your branch, you are committing on the front end to make the branch successful. This may involve renting an office space, getting a local phone number, putting the branch location on your website, etc. From day one, you want to be seen as a "local" company vying for business.

Strengths of This Method

This method is very attractive to a company focused on gaining a strong presence in a certain geography. If your goal is very targeted growth in certain markets (as opposed to certain types of accounts in any geography), then this method can make a lot of sense. When you "commit" to a market by hiring managers, getting office space, etc., it gets easier and easier to acquire new customers. Prospects leery of out-of-towners will be more likely to see you as local. We have found this approach to be very successful in mid-sized markets where the competition is weak. The other benefit to this approach is that it lets you start growth immediately by targeting smaller accounts. You can gain a presence in an area within a few months through $1,000-$5,000/month accounts.

Weaknesses of This Method

This method of growth has two downsides in my opinion. First, by going all-in in a certain geography, you run the risk of that branch not being successful in the long run due to stiff competition. While your operation may be strong, you may have strong competition that has a big share of the market. This could result in much financial bleeding for many years. The second downside is that you will lose money for a period of time. Our experience shows that you will likely be in the red for a period of 6-24 months. However, when compared to opportunity costs of not growing, this is a fairly reasonable tradeoff from a risk perspective, as the losses incurred are usually very small.

Description: Acquisition

Next, I want to discuss what many would consider the sexiest way to grow, acquisition. Acquisitions, or the purchase of another company, is something you read about frequently in the news, even in our own industry. For instance, ABM recently purchased GCA in an effort to gain a greater market share in the education sector. There is no doubt that acquisition can be a great way to grow, and grow fast. But is it right for you? While this is an incredibly complex topic, let's break it down into three parts: the reasons for acquisition, the potential downsides, and whether or not an acquisition is right for you.

The Reasons For Acquisition

In our industry, reasons for acquisition can vary, but generally they can be lumped under the following three categories: accelerate growth, enter a new geographic market, or enter a new vertical market. Most experts say, and I agree, that accelerated growth is a terrible reason to acquire a company. While growth is always an outcome of acquisition, if not tied to entry into a new market (whether geographic or vertical), then it is ill-advised. As mentioned in the previous posts, entering a new market is tough. Often it takes business to get business, so if you don't have a school but want to get into the education sector, that can be a huge hurdle. The same could be said of a new geographic location. An acquisition can give you an immediate foothold.

The Potential Downsides

The biggest downside is that statistically speaking, most acquisitions are failures. They usually do not provide the ROI desired, and growth via another method would have been better. Second, acquisition typically requires a strong cash position, something many companies don't have. Most deals in the cleaning industry involve three layers of financing: bank, seller, and buyer cash. You need be ready to shell out 20%-30% of the deal in cash. So, for instance, if you are buying a $1M company with a 10% EBITDA and a selling multiple of 5x, then the overall purchase price of the company would be $500k. Assuming you needed 30% down in cash, this would be $150,000. Finally, one of the biggest reasons for acquisition failure is culture fit. For those of you with blended families, imagine putting $500k on the line, requiring everyone to get along and work together, and you get the idea.

Is An Acquisition Right for You?

Let me offer three guidelines for determining whether or not an acquisition is right for you – three questions to ask yourself.

- Do you need to break into a new market and cannot make it happen via organic growth?
- Do you have the cash necessary to make the deal and COMFORTABLY continue your current operation?
- Can you identify a company of the right size and culture fit?

If you can confidently answer "Yes" to the first two questions, then I would suggest speaking with an M&A consultant.

15

Why Habits Give Freedom and Encourage Growth

This morning, you got in your car and backed out of your driveway and headed to work. No big deal, right? Well, yes and no. You have done this so many times now that you don't think twice about the process. But think for a second back to when you first began driving and let's walk through every step of the process. You walk out the door and get into your car. You adjust the seat, you put your seatbelt on. You put the key in the ignition, press the brake, and start the car. You keep your foot on the brake, put the car in reverse, and then begin looking in your side view and rear-view mirrors over and over. You slowly start backing out, frantically looking in every mirror to ensure you aren't running into the yard or hitting something.

When you first began driving, the mental concentration was immense. But now, a seasoned driver, you don't think twice about hopping in the car and backing out of the driveway. This process has now moved into your subconscious and requires almost no mental effort. You can now focus on other things like thinking about your day, listening to the radio, etc. So, what do this have to do with your BSC? Everything!

When you don't have systems (i.e. habits or routines) in place, the mental and emotional energy required to keep things running is immense. You frantically run from task to task and place to place putting out fires. At the end of the week, you are exhausted, physically, and mentally, yet your company is in no better place than when the week started. You have made zero progress toward scaling up and giving yourself more freedom as an owner.

To find relief from this rat race, you need habits in your company. You need standard ways of doing business that move tasks from the conscious to the subconscious mind of your business. Hiring and onboarding should require less and less energy because everyone knows how the system works. Quality control should get easier and easier (and customers should be happier) because everyone is following the same steps to ensure it happens.

A company without systems is a company that creates stress and shackles its leaders to the daily grind. A cleaning company without processes is a people dependent company and not a system dependent company. And people dependent companies are less valuable, more stressful, less effective, and more difficult to scale.

If you want freedom, more profits, and a chance to grow and scale up, you must have company habits. Freedom awaits, but the door only opens to those who systematize much of what they do. It's your choice.

16

Five Tips to Make Your BSC Sellable

Regardless of the stage of life you are in, positioning your BSC for a potential sale should always be something on your mind. As I speak with BSC owners around the country, most are looking to exit the business at some point and of those, most are looking to fund their retirement through this exit process. So whether you want to pass the business on to family or employees or just sell outright, you should be doing things now to make your company as valuable as possible when that exit inevitably comes. For purposes of this article, we will focus on the keys to building value in hopes of selling to a larger BSC or other individual outside

How purchase price is determined
Whether you are selling to another BSC, an employee, a family member, or an outsider to the industry, the way to calculate the sale price is the same. Nearly all buyers are going to be willing to pay a multiple of yearly EBITDA (Earnings Before Interest, Taxes, Depreciation, & Amortization). In the

BSC industry, this multiplier is usually between 3x and 6x, depending upon several factors. The more desirable the company and smaller the risk, the higher the multiplier. So, for instance, if you have a $5M company with a 10% EBITDA ($500k profit) and your risk profile is low, then you could expect a 4x or 5x multiplier. This multiplier would translate into a purchase price of $2M or $2.5M.

BSC owners should position their company to maximize the multiplier. Here are five ways you can make that happen.

Sales Multiplier Tip #1

The first tip to maximize sales price is to have a niche. There is an old saying that is certainly true: "the riches are in the niches." When you have a niche, you have more specialty; therefore, your strategic position is stronger. Niches can be related to geography, service type, customer type, etc. But know this, if you will do everything for everyone, you don't have a niche and your value is likely lower. If everyone is your customer, no one is your customer. Pick a niche, stick to it, and you will find a buyer looking specifically for that niche. When a buyer really wants you, you can demand a higher purchase price.

Sales Multiplier Tip #2

While this is perhaps the most controversial of all the tips, I am convinced it is largely true. The larger your accounts, the more attractive your business will be to a potential suitor, especially another BSC. Larger accounts offer a host of benefits. First, because of their size, there are many ways profits can be improved (labor reduction, supply savings, extra-bill services, etc). This gives the buyer "upside" which makes you more attractive. Second, large accounts are less complex from an organizational standpoint, requiring less overhead to maintain. The headache factor is less when you have one large account vs. thirty small accounts. Third, larger accounts are more easily managed from afar, making them more attractive to an out-of-town purchaser or absentee owner. Finally, large accounts generally have less competition from smaller janitorial contractors, making the likelihood of losing them less. For these reasons and more, having larger accounts will help you get a larger sales multiplier.

Sales Multiplier Tip #3

Being able to function without the direct, daily involvement of the owner is critical in maximizing your sales multiplier. When a company relies heavily on the involvement of its owner, it will be in a vulnerable position once the owner is absent. This is an obvious risk for any potential purchaser, one that will certainly drive down the purchase price. To limit this risk, you must begin positioning your company to run without you. The upside to this move is that while you are making your company more valuable, you are at the same time giving yourself more freedom.

Sales Multiplier Tip #4

Having been involved in the acquisition process myself, I can attest that "clean financials" are a really big deal. When a person is looking to acquire a business, the financials (and specifically the profit), are the primary consideration. In order to accurately assess the financial position of the company, accurate financial statements are *critical.* When a potential buyer can't make heads or tails of the numbers, the inherent risk greatly increases. Clean and specific financials, clear of personal expenses, along with periodic audits from a CPA will give buyers a comfort level needed to make a strong offer. Messy financials will have the opposite effect, driving down the sales multiplier.

Sales Multiplier Tip #5

The final tip is broad but equally important - lower risk wherever possible. Risk is a key driver to the sales multiplier. The lower the risk, the higher the multiplier - the higher the risk the lower the multiplier. There are several ways you can lower risk and make your company more attractive to a potential buyer. Here are a few key risk-reducing items:

- Ensure that all accounts are contractually secure and relationships are strong. Ideally, you have other managers in your company who have strong relationships with your key clients.
- Do not have more than 25% of your business with one customer. Over-leveraging yourself with one or two clients is a recipe for disaster. Work diligently to spread risk out over many customers.
- Show a track record of growth for the last few years. This shows that you are not positioned to lose business, but rather upside exists and can be realized quickly.

Conclusion

You may not be looking to get out of the business right now or even in the near future. I understand that. However, it is never too early to begin positioning your company for when that day comes. The process can take longer than you realize and your desire to sell may change sooner than you think. An added bonus to the above tips is that they increase your profits, make your company more stable, and give you more freedom as an owner. It truly is a win-win.

Sales & Marketing

17

Cleaning and Production Rates

A question I often get is: "How should I bid this job?" Given that the two biggest line items on any budget are labor and overhead/profit, what is usually meant by the original question is how many cleaning labor hours should I figure for this job. Since graduating from Civil Engineering school, I have been bidding on jobs from $5,000 to $10,000,000 in size in a few different industries. No matter the industry, this is the perennial question: "What is it going to take to do the job?" For janitorial companies, this is a labor production rate question. Let me offer three ways to answer this "*how much*" question.

Industry Production Averages

The ISSA and other groups have produced standard cleaning rates for a variety of cleaning tasks. For instance, restroom fixtures on average take 2 to 3 minutes to clean. Vacuuming can be done at a rate of 8,000 sf/hr or more. Using these standard rates, one can break down a building into the various areas and then calculate the time it would take to perform the necessary tasks. The downside to using standard rates is that they are just an average and radically differ from building to building depending upon a host of factors. So, while this is a good place to start, you should not bank your bid on such rates.

Your Company Averages

A much better method of predicting your production rates is to look at existing customers and figure your own internal production rates. While you may not break down task by task production rates, you will be able to assess production rates of general areas or building types. For instance, you may find that medium density office buildings clean at a rate of 4500 sqft/hr whereas high-density, cubicle filled office buildings clean at a rate of 3500 sqft/hr. Knowing your own internal labor production rates will give you a great starting point for bidding a new job.

Gut Feeling

Every good estimator has a certain level of intuition when it comes to their craft. This is not some rash conclusion or lazy bidding effort, but a real intuition of what it takes to get the job done. Experienced estimators with many successful projects under their belt may not be able to put into words the reasons for their bid modifications, but nonetheless their hunches usually turn out right. The more you bid, the better your intuition will become.

It is my suggestion that you build your production rates upon your company averages then modify those rates on a case-by-case basis as your bidding experience increases. Let the numbers be your guide.

18

How Much Should You Mark Up Your Bids?

I often get asked, "How should I price my jobs? How can I bid in such a way that I'm profitable, yet don't price myself out of the job?" Assuming the prospect likes you and your company, this is the *key* question that must be answered. Do you bid based on price per square foot? Do you find out the budget then make it work? How much do you mark up your costs? Let me offer three suggestions for pricing your cleaning jobs.

Know Your Numbers

I can't tell you how many people I talk to in the industry that don't really know their costs or production rates. But when you are bidding on new jobs, there are essentially two key things that affect your price, labor, and supplies. You must know how long it takes you to clean each type of building you service. How many square feet per hour can you clean medium density offices? How long do plant restrooms take you to clean per fixture? To get these numbers, let me suggest you go out in the field and time your team in a variety of settings to gather this info. Second, look at all of your existing buildings and find the average time it takes to clean each one. These two methods should give you enough data to get a good handle on your company's cleaning rate. The same tactics would apply to your supply's expense. Use history to determine future expenses.

Know Your Customer's Budget

Ok, I know this sounds crazy, but it is really helpful to know approximately what the customer is currently paying or what they are hoping to pay. You can build a Cadillac or Pinto budget for the customer, but knowing their price expectation level helps you determine which is best. Remember, "clean" is a subjective term and expectations can vary wildly from customer to customer. Ask questions such as, "What is your approximate annual budget for cleaning services" or "Do you have a number you are trying to stay under." These sorts of questions help you know how to build your program.

Mark Up Based On Size And Desire To Get The Job

If you know your costs well and you have a general idea of where the customer wants to be financially, you can now finagle with the markup. As a general rule, markup ranges from 15% to 50%, depending upon the size of the job. Smaller jobs get a higher markup and larger jobs get a smaller markup. At the end of the day, you must decide how much you are willing to make (as a dollar amount) for the work, management, and financial risk you are taking.

19

Compensating Sales Reps

I am often asked the question, "How should I compensate my sales rep?" Janitorial business owners want to see their business grow at a faster rate, but they lack the time to make it happen. Therefore, they turn to hiring a sales rep. But many are unsure how to pay in such a way that promotes success. How can they develop a compensation plan that attracts good candidates, but also promotes and ensures the kind of sales you want in your business? I have personally seen sales compensation plans that created apathetic sales reps and others that accidentally encouraged the wrong type of sales. So let me offer three suggestions for crafting that perfect sales compensation plan.

Base Salary

With any base salary, there is a narrow road with ditches on both sides. The first ditch is a base salary that is so low that it will not attract the caliber of individual you want. Sure, a good sales rep will be able to make his/her living on commission if necessary, but a salary too low shows little trust in the person. Additionally, there can be dry spells in the commercial cleaning industry, and you want your team to know you've got their back. The other ditch is to pay the sales rep too much where he/she is not sufficiently motivated to make more sales. In my experience in the industry, the sweet spot for a base salary is somewhere between $45k and $65k per year along with a good benefits package.

Sales Commission

At the end of the day, ongoing profit is the end goal of sales. Therefore, you want to pay commission that is tied to new account profitability. If commission is tied to revenue, number of sales, or some other metric, you could incentivize behavior that is detrimental to the company. My suggestion is to pay a multiple of the budgeted monthly profit, with the stipulation that operations approves of the budget before the sale is made. A multiple of 1.5x – 3x is appropriate, depending upon the base salary. For commercial cleaning companies trying to hit between $500k – $1M in new sales per year, this should amount to $20k-$50k in sales commission.

Commission Structure

The final step to a good sales compensation plan is a commission structure. This is the rules and regulations portion of the commission plan. For instance, you only want to pay commission on certain types of jobs. So you may pay zero commission for residential or retail jobs if those are jobs you don't want to pursue. Another component of the commission structure is the payout. I recommend that sales commission doesn't start getting paid out until the first check from the customer comes in. Additionally, commission should be spread out over a period of 3-6 months so the sales rep has some vested interest in ensuring the accounts gets off to a good start.

20

Find Prospects Without Leaving the Office

What if I told you that you could find every possible prospect you wanted to pursue without ever leaving your office? What if I said that you didn't need to network, attend social events, or drive around in order to identify the commercial cleaning accounts you wanted to market to? I know this may sound pie in the sky, but trust me, this is the new method of prospecting. In the cleaning world, gone are the days of driving for dollars. With the mountains of information at our fingertips, a few simple online research tools can help you build a robust prospect list for less than $200. Let me give you the four main tools I use – and don't forget to watch the free janitorial prospecting course linked below.

Resource #1 – List Building Websites

List building websites are the first place to go when building your prospect list. Sites like Hoovers and InfoUSA are storehouses of B2B information. You can define your ideal client profile, enter your search criteria, and BAM! For less than $1.00/lead, you can purchase entire excel spreadsheet of your ideal clients along with addresses, phone numbers, and names of key employees. If you don't have a robust prospect list, start here.

Resource #2 – Google Maps

I know it sounds crazy, but Google Maps is an amazing resource for finding new prospects. Go to the area you want to prospect in, switch to aerial view, and start looking for large buildings and parking lots. When you click on a specific building, Google will often give you information such as the company name, address, and phone number. Additionally, you can switch to Street View and "drive around" from your computer, looking at the view from the road.

Resource #3 – Chamber of Commerce & Economic Development Websites

Most cities, counties, states, or metropolitan areas have chamber of commerce or economic development websites. These sites often contain information about employers in the area. At the very least, you can often find lists of the largest employers in the area along with news about new employers who have recently moved into the market.

Resource #4 – Niche Websites & Directories

Finally, when you are searching for schools, medical facilities, or other such facilities, you can often find free lists on niche websites. For instance, there are many websites on the state level that contain lists of private schools along with contact information. Likewise, many groups are dedicated to surgery centers, nursing homes, or other niche medical facilities. These websites are home to much free information to help you finalize your prospect list.

21

You're Asking the Wrong Question

Do you ever wonder why your marketing efforts seem average at best? Do you spend time making calls, sending emails, and delivering brochures only to be met with disinterest? Have you spent thousands on telemarketing companies or marketing gurus only to see little return? Are you convinced that selling is purely a numbers and luck game? If you answered yes, then you are asking the wrong question.

The key question in marketing is not "What do I do?" Rather, it is "Who do I serve." Most business owners are proud of the service they deliver to their clients. They spend years perfecting their hiring processes, their customer retention methods, and their quality control procedures. They very well may offer the highest quality service in the market. But being the best will not help you win the marketing game. In fact, the prospect doesn't really care about all of your fancy programs and processes. They care about themselves and their needs.

As sales and marketing professionals in the BSC industry, the one ego smashing reality we must accept is that most customers don't really care about the cleaning. They really don't! Sure, they want a clean building and no complaints, but they are not genuinely interested in the cleaning program itself.

However, what is the #1 thing we try to do to get their attention? We tell them how great we are and how awesome our people and processes are. To attract the genuine attention of your prospect, you need to reorient the conversation, making it about the needs and desires of the client. How do they currently feel? How do they want to feel? What outcome are they looking for? What is their ultimate goal in having a cleaning company?

The 5 Why's Challenge

Let me leave you with this challenge. Go and meet with four or five of your largest and best clients and ask them the series of questions below. However, don't just accept their first answer. Ask "why" five times. With each answer, ask "why." Then do it again with their next answer until you feel convinced that you have gotten to the real root of their answer. Here are the questions to ask:

- What are you looking for in a janitorial contractor?
- Why did you choose our company?

- What are the things that you spend most of your time on?
- What are the things that you spend most of your emotional energy on?
- How do you feel when the janitorial service is going really well?
- How do you feel when there are issues with the service?

Once you get these answers, you will be in a much better position to begin a truly effective marketing program.

22

Three Steps to Land Large Accounts

If you are serious about scaling up your BSC company, you must focus on landing larger accounts. On average, these accounts offer significantly more profit for the effort involved compared to a cluster of smaller accounts totaling the same monthly revenue. They are the stepping stones to reaching the next plateau of growth. While it can be hard to say "No" to prospective clients, this may in fact be the quickest way to move your company forward. As Harvard's Michael Porter says, "Strategy is more about learning to say, 'No' and less about saying, 'Yes.'"

In this article, I want to offer some suggestions for how you can find and land these large accounts. Now for those of you that are smaller, I know you can struggle with feelings of inadequacy and inferiority. "How can I compete with those larger companies?" "What chance do I really have of landing a large account when I'm just a small local company?" But fear not! This process is easier than you might think and your chances are greater than you might think. You just need the guts to go out and make it happen!

The first step to getting large accounts is finding large accounts. And trust me, this is not complicated. There are basically three ways to identify large account prospects in your market.

Develop a list of the largest employers in your area

Depending on your definition of "large", employee counts of at least 300 (on one site) have the greatest chance of being an ideal prospect. Remember, the more people traffic a facility has, the greater the cleaning and maintenance needs. Lists can be built through a variety of sources:

Paid list sites (Hoovers, InfoUSA, etc.)

Local/state chamber and economic development websites

- Google Maps aerial views. (Look for large parking lots with numerous cars)

Cold call to mine for information to ensure the prospect truly is a large account

You never want to expend a tremendous amount of sales energy until you are sure the account is truly a "large" prospect. Here are a few questions to help you ascertain the size of the account. Don't worry if you can't get all the answers.

- How many employees work at your facility?
- Do you outsource the janitorial service?
- Do they clean the whole building or just part of it?

- How many cleaners are on the cleaning staff?
- What shifts do the cleaners works?

Find the decision maker

Nothing wastes more time that selling to a person who is not the ultimate decision maker. If the true account decision maker is not sold on your company, your chances of winning the bid are small. Selling 101 says to find the key decision maker(s) FIRST.

Project A Confident, Competent, "Big Company" Image

To sell an account, you must garner the trust of the decision maker. Unless they believe you are confident and competent to do the work, they will be unwilling to give you a shot. And how can you expect them to trust in your company if you don't believe in yourself and project an air of confidence about your company's abilities. To get a seat at the bargaining table, you must help the decision maker believe you are a viable possibility. Here are a few tips.

- Use the word "regional" instead of "local" to discuss your company's geographic reach.
- Get reference letters from customers in similar industries even if they are smaller in size. For instance, a good reference from a $5,000/month manufacturing client can help you land a $10,000/month manufacturing client.

- Talk about your management team using more official "corporate" language. If you have a couple of people in your office who handle hiring and paperwork, call them "the HR team" and not "Jane and Tim in the office." You don't want the prospect to see you as an owner operator (which is a risky choice). Rather, they want a qualified company with a high-caliber team.

- Large corporate clients speak a certain language, and speaking that language is important. So for instance, instead of saying "we will check to make sure the cleaning work is done right," talk about your "quality control program." The shift in verbiage is subtle, but the impact is significant I believe.

While these tips are by no means exhaustive, they give you a picture of the ways your marketing efforts can impact the prospect's perception of your BSC.

Big Enough, Small Enough – Your Sales Pitch To Beat The Big Boys

The final tip I have for you is by far my personal favorite – one we've used to consistently win bids over and against our larger competitors. As a small or midsized, professional janitorial contractor, you have a unique advantage over your larger competitors. You likely have all the capabilities to service the account just as well as your larger peers; however, you are small enough to deliver a relationship that few larger companies can offer.

As the owner of your BSC, consider the impact of sliding a business card across the table to the prospect and saying the following. "Mr. Prospect, I am the owner and president of ABC Janitorial. If we are fortunate enough to gain your business, you will instantly become a top 5 client of ours. Because of this, you will get a level of attention that few other companies can offer. You have my personal guarantee (and my cell number if ever needed) that this account will be a success. We are large enough to handle all of your building service needs, but small enough to offer you a level of service you won't get anywhere else." That, friends, is a sales pitch that works!

23

How to Calculate Strip & Wax and Sell a Lot of It

Stripping and waxing resilient floors can be a very profitable form of extra-bill work if priced correctly, sometimes bringing in profit margins north of 50%. Not only is this work very profitable, it makes routine floor maintenance easier and can drastically improve the look of the customer's facility. Most of us use standard per square foot prices when we submit pricing to our customers. However, understanding how this price is derived can help us make modifications when necessary and give us more confidence when pricing larger or more complicated jobs.

Below is a strip and wax pricing example given to me by Tom Wilkinson, a friend, long-time industry veteran, and a fellow member of the Elite BSC Mastermind Group.

Example - Strip and Wax 10,000sf VCT

- Cost of stripper (10,000 sq ft / 1,000 sq ft per gallon = 10 gallons x $15 = ($150) = 1.5 cents per square foot

- Cost of finish (5 coats x 10,000 sq ft / 2000 sq ft per gallon = 25 gallons x $14ea = $350) = $.035 cents per square foot ($350)
- Cost of pads, mops, etc. (estimate) = 1.5 cents per square foot ($150.00)
- Cost of labor (2 people, 2500 sq feet per day to strip and finish, 4 total days @ 8 hours each (64 total hrs), $18 per hour wages, + 20% for taxes and insurance = $1,382) = $.14 cents per square foot *This figure could go up or down depending upon the difficulty of the job*

Total costs to contractor = $0.20 per square foot or $2032.00 cost for labor and material, not including travel or moving of furniture.

Here are the final prices to the customer, based on various markup amounts.

- 50% Markup - $0.30/sf
- 75% Markup - $0.35/sf
- 100% Markup - $0.40/sf

By keeping an eye on your material and labor prices, you can keep maintain a firm grasp on your strip and wax costs.

The Best Way to Increase Floor Work Sales

In my experience, an active approach to extra bill sales is far more successful than waiting for customers to call and request services. And the best way to employ an active approach to add sales is using the managers most closely connected to the customers. Additionally, pay commission on all add-work sold.

At my company, we give all our area managers the authority to sell extra bill projects to their customers. They know the building needs and they have regular access to the customer. Armed with a standard price sheet and the motivation of gaining sales commission, our managers are well positioned to sell extra-bill work. In the past 3 years, we have doubled the amount of extra bill work we do by deploying our area managers in this manner.

Know your pricing, empower your managers, and pay them commission. This is the recipe for extra-bill success.

24

Bigger Accounts: The Key to Scaling Up

One of the most common questions I receive as a BSC consultant is "How can I grow my business to 2x, 3x, or 5x my current size within the next three to five years?" Sometimes the question is posed a different way. "How can I get to $3 million or $5 million in revenue over the next 5 years so I can have the option of selling my business?" Regardless of the size, every cleaning business owner is asking this question. We all have our reasons to grow. For some it's money, for other it's the ability to have a sellable company, yet others want to diversify and limit risk.

Regardless of the reason, we all want the same outcome — growth. Now wanting growth and getting growth are two different animals. Getting the growth you want to achieve your goals can be a daunting task, a task the often turns would-be growers into always-wishing-never-acting stallers. But it doesn't have to be that way. In fact, growth is much easier than you think if you have the correct plan in place.

And I want to share with you what that plan should look like. The key? *Think big!*

Case Study

John has a janitorial company doing $1 million in revenue per year, operating in a market of 300k people with a few smaller towns within a 1-hour drive. His $1M in revenue is comprised of accounts ranging in size from $250/month to $5,000/month, with most being under $1,500/month. For John, it has taken him 10+ years to grow his business to this point. In order for him to reach his goal of $4M in the next five years, he must change the way he looks at sales. Put another way, he must redefine his ideal client.

If his average account size is $1,200/month, simple math shows that he would need 208 new accounts, or 3.5 new accounts per month, assuming ZERO lost business. If you have done any sort of selling in this industry, you know that is a tough goal to hit. His past track record would indicate this is not possible. Even harder than hitting the sales goal would be servicing 208 DIFFERENT new customers in order to make that $4M in revenue. So, what must John do?

In order for John to hit his 5-year revenue goal, he must redefine has ideal customer and put a laser focus on targeting those customers. If John's new ideal customer were 3x his current average size (or $3,600/month), he would only need to close 1.2 accounts per month and would only end up with 70 new customers – certainly a much more attainable goal. But what if John thought even bigger, and targeted only account $5k/month and greater?

By only targeting prospects $5k/month and greater, John would reduce total new clients to 50 over the course of 5 years, which is less than one new client per month. From an operational and sales standpoint, this is a very manageable number. And from our experience (at Frantz Building Services), a company can achieve roughly $1M-$1.5M in revenue per 100k in metropolitan area population.

Change Your Strategy

So, for those of you wanting to scale up your business to achieve your long-term goals, you must change the way you think about growth. As the old saying goes, "What got you here won't get you there." To get larger revenues in a shorter amount of time, you must start thinking bigger – you must start expecting bigger. I promise you, the business is there! Your job is to identify it and go get it. Here is a short table of the account sizes you should be chasing if you want to scale up. The sizes of ideal prospects vary depending on janitorial company size.

Janitorial Company Size	Ideal Prospect Size
$500k - $1M	$2,000-$7,000/mo
$1M-$3M	$3,000-$12,000/mo
$3M-$6M	$5,000-$20,000/mo
$6M-$10M	$8,000-$70,000/mo

What got you here won't get you there. You need to reorient your thinking on growing your business. You need to start THINKING BIG!

25

Five Reasons to Say "No" to a Prospective Customer

As building service contractors, we are always looking for ways to grow our business. We want to scale up, increase our freedom, and build a great business. However, this desire can often make us think about nothing other than sales. We think that getting new business is the key and the details will get worked out later. However, to our own detriment, we forget to place boundaries around our sales process. We indiscriminately say, "Yes" to every opportunity that comes our way and sales soon becomes a barrier to future success.

As Michael Porter once said in a Harvard Business Review article, "Strategy is often more about learning when to say no." I think Porter is exactly right. A carefully run organization should never be sacrificed on the altar of indiscriminate growth. While turning down business is painful (trust me, I know), it can be the best decision for your company. The obvious question you are asking is: "When do I say no?"

Here are the five primary reasons to say no to a prospective customer.

#1 - The Account Is Too Small

Every janitorial contractor that starts out must begin with smaller contracts. You initially don't have the capital or the experience to start large projects, and small jobs are a great way to get your feet wet. However, it is difficult to build a large, scalable company on these types of accounts. As you grow, you must begin saying NO to these smaller accounts. While the margins can be good, remember that smaller customer take just as much time/energy to service as large customers, sometimes even more. So, for instance, a $500 customer, while maybe boasting a 50% profit margin, can sound good, a $5,000 customer at 30% profit makes a lot more sense. The time/energy is the same in servicing the account but the actual profit dollar difference is significant. While you may be able to handle both for a period of time, you don't ever want the smaller jobs hindering your ability to service larger, more profitable customers.

Now don't get me wrong, these smaller customers need a good contractor to support them, but a smaller janitorial contractor is better suited to make that happen. If you truly want to scale up your company, you must institute a cutoff for smaller customers. For my company, that cutoff has changed over time. It used to be $500/month, then $750/month, and now it is at $1,500/month.

#2 – The Account Is Too Large

This one hurts! Sometimes an account is just too large for you to reasonably handle. Accounts that are too large can cause several problems for you. First, they can put a severe strain on your cash flow by forcing you to front large amounts of capital to get the job started. Remember, businesses don't go under for lack of profitability, but lack of cash. Second, large jobs can put your company in a risky situation by having you over-leveraged with a single customer. I would never let one customer account for more than 30% of my business. Finally, accounts too large can tie up your resources and hinder your ability to service other customers well. In doing so, you will jeopardize your entire business for the sake of one customer. This is never a good idea.

#3 – The Account Is Too Far Away

Most of us have faced the decision of servicing an account just outside of our normal service territory. My rule of thumb is this: if you don't plan to grow in that new area, then don't pick up the account. Successfully managing accounts requires active and present management. When an account is more than an hour away, it can eat up nearly an entire day for a manager to make a stop. This not only pulls your manager away from other important accounts, but also makes him / her reluctant to visit this far-away new customer. If you are not careful, an account too far away can become a drain on your entire business. If you are not confident and excited to take on the new account, then don't do it. Remember, smart & planned growth is better.

#4 – The Customer Only Cares About Price

This perhaps may be the toughest of all to deal with. We all know this type of customer. They only care about the bottom line. They switch contractors every two or three years in an effort to keep the price low. Somehow, we think we will be the exception to the rule, the contractor they will decide to keep for many years. But don't be fooled, past action is the best predictor of the future. If a customer only cares about price and has a history of changing contractors, then stay away. You are looking for long-term relationships, not get-in, get out contracts. Here are a few hints that price is the only consideration:

- The prospect has had 3 or more contractors in the last 5 years.
- The prospect will not let you give an in-person sales presentation.
- The prospect will not sign an agreement longer than one year.
- The prospect does not care about quality control, partnership meetings, etc.

#5 – The Customer Type Doesn't Fit

This final reason to say no is not always so easy to figure out. How can you know which customers are not a good fit? My suggestion is this: look at your existing customer base and see if the new prospect looks similar in terms of how they are serviced. Are the hours similar? The expectations? The services? To give an example, my company is focused on larger commercial office and manufacturing facilities. However, we took a stab at servicing big box retailers. The hours were totally different and required management at hours when we didn't have managers working. Very quickly, we realized it was a terrible fit for our company and we of the account.

It Is Never Cut and Dry

Knowing when to say no is rarely an easy decision. We often struggle when we are on the fence about the decision. The account is slightly too large or slightly too far away. Or maybe the niche is totally different, but you think it could open up a door for you to grow the business. The key is this: saying no is a good thing, sometimes the best thing. Make some rules for you and your team and stick to them. These rules will help you know when to say, "Yes" and help you avoid situations that put your company at risk. Smart, controlled growth is better than fast, indiscriminate growth.

26

Customers Buy Intangibles, So Stop Selling Products

In the early part of the 21st century the airline industry suffered devastating blows. Numerous companies filed for bankruptcy while others simply faded from existence. But one company continued (and continues) to rise above the crowd and produce profits year after year. This company is increasingly becoming the market leader in the airline industry. This company is Southwest Airlines (SWA). SWA has been the most profitable airline company since 1973. What differentiates SWA from its competitors is not its products, but its service differentiation. Every airline has nice airplanes; some I would dare say are even better than SWA's airplanes. But SWA understands that it is not a product company, but rather a service company. And because of this fundamental understanding, they have chosen for themselves a niche in the airline service industry. They are a no-frills transportation company determined to give you a fun flight at a cheap price. That is it! When I think of SWA that is what pops into my mind. The same holds true for other successful service companies. Domino's Pizza...fast delivery. Pizza Hut...great tasting pizza. Little Caesars...Hot-n-Ready pizza. These companies have products, but they make themselves market leaders by delivering an intangible experience to the customer, and this experience is what makes the customer choose them over their competitors.

Many of us in the service industry want to wow our prospective customers with our "products" and "methodologies." To quote Market Leadership Strategies for Service Companies, "The majority tends to err on the side of overemphasizing and promoting the tangibles while almost ignoring the intangibles...While methodologies are good for promoting quality, they are unhelpful and often damaging for companies pursuing differentiation. A service is an experience that customers feel and remember. The other physical senses do not come into play as they do with products." In my industry, janitorial services, it is difficult to differentiate yourself from the thousands of competitors in the market, and so often you resort to talking about your "superior equipment, quality control measures, and products." But at the end of the day, has there really been a perceived difference in my service and that of my competitor? And if there is no perceived difference, then the prospect is going to make a decision based upon price. In order to break away from this vicious, profit-minimizing cycle, you *must be different.* You do not need to "get better" and "become more efficient." This only prolongs the rat race you are in with your competitors.

So how can you do this? How can you set yourself apart from your competitors? How can you be different, yet wildly successful with a particular customer base? To begin this process, you must start with your customer. Identify your top customers and identify prospects that you would like to become your customers. Meet with these individuals in what I call "focus groups" to find out why these customers like your service. What is it about your company that causes them to stay with you? You might be surprised at their response. In addition to finding out what they like about your company, find out what they wish they had in a service company. What needs do they have? What could you provide to ease their pain? What would make their job easier? Ask lots of questions. Learn your prospect. The answers to these questions will be the starting point for building your organization to become a market leader.

You will never be successful as a service company until you know what it is that your customer wants. Find out what they want and then find a way to market and deliver that service in a way that is completely distinct from your competition. Only then will you begin to move through the uncharted waters of successful market leadership. Swallow your pride and open the door to the possibility that the way you have been doing things in the past may not be what will make you successful in the future.

27

Avoid the "Be Better" Trap

Does your company strive and strain to be better than your competitors? To rise above your competition? To outshine the company next door? If you do, then you are not alone, and I would even say that this is a normal, healthy feeling for your company. But as business owners and managers, we must be careful that we do not fall into the "be better" trap. This trap that has us pitted against rival companies can potentially cause us to ignore our customers wants and needs in the vain effort of trying to outperform our competitors. So, are you a "be better" kind of company? Take the following test.

Give yourself a score of 1–5 on each of the following six descriptions. The higher your score, the more likely you are a "be better" company.

- Lately, customers seem to select only according to price.

- Customers no longer value our sales force.
- Our new services and products are copied within months or have been copied from other competitors by us.
- Customers don't attach any benefits to our company's brand.
- Marketing and innovation play second fiddle to operations.
- Our salespeople can't articulate what distinguishes us from competitors.

So how did you do? For those of you "be better" companies, let's look at a couple of the potential causes. One potential problem is that you may be focusing too much on refining your operations, trying to standardize things a bit too much. Now don't get me wrong, standardization is very important and necessary, especially for small businesses. It is critical for growth that you have a system for doing business. But the problem lies when all of our efforts are placed in improving our operation and little to no effort is placed into innovation. To quote the Terrill and Middlebrooks, "Management falls into a trap – they convince themselves that all of their efforts and investments to improve internal operations and be slightly better than competitors will also produce new value for customers. In reality, customers often respond through their purchasing habits with a bored 'Who cares?'"

Maybe you are not trying to standardize too much, but perhaps you are trying to emulate your competitors. Customers do not want a better XYZ company; they want something different than XYZ. If you cannot distinguish yourself from XYZ, then your customer is going to make his/her decision based upon price. You must have differentiators! I don't buy from Chick-fil-A because they have the best chicken nuggets and fries, but because I have the best service experience of any fast-food restaurant in the industry. Can your customers say something about you that is different than all your competition?

So, what can you do? Talk to your customers. What do they want and need? What are their hot buttons? What are their pain points? Get to know your customer and the prospects you would like to be your customer. Once you know them, then create services and solutions to meet their needs.

Operations

28

Five Tips For Partnership Meetings

Strong relationships with customers are key to making your janitorial company a success. And while good service is essential, a relationship built on trust and communication will ensure a long partnership. But how can you keep your relationships strong? Knowing that surface-level conversations and responding to complaints aren't enough, how can you make your customer meetings effective? How can you turn customer interactions into retention and profit increasing sessions? Let me offer five tips for a slam-dunk partnership meeting.

Make Them Regular and Scheduled

Partnership meetings with customers should be held monthly or quarterly. Sporadic meetings are a bad look, but pre-planned, scheduled meetings model consistency and professionalism. They indicate to the customer you are proactive and take their account seriously. But don't rely on the customer to take initiative. It is your job to plan the meetings, ensure attendance, and drive the agenda.

Have An Agenda

Don't *ever* walk into your meetings and ask, "How is everything going?" Rather, have an agenda that works through specific talking points and addresses relevant issues. Personal conversation, quality, upcoming needs, issues, past successes, etc. should be addressed each time.

Include A Quality Score

During each partnership meeting, you want to ask the customer to give you a performance score using a 1-5 or 1-10 scale. Additionally, you want to ask them specifically what you can do in the upcoming month(s) to improve your score. This not only gives you a regular gauge of your standing with the customer, but it specifically helps you see how to improve. Finally, this quality score helps keep the customer grounded in the event of a future service failure. Reminding the customer of past scores can help them see your consistent service success.

Reinforce Value

Operations is actually in the business of selling to existing customers. You must constantly sell (or remind) your customers of the value they are receiving from your cleaning company. How have you reduced complaints? What extra services have you performed? Given that our industry is often complaint driven, you must remind the customer regularly what you do for them.

Up-sell

Last but not least, you need to constantly be looking for ways to up-sell your customers. Delivering more services to your customers makes you and your company more valuable and indispensable. A company that just cleans is easy to replace. A company that cleans, supplies consumable products, power-washes the sidewalks, cleans the windows, and handles the recycle program is much harder to replace. Add value by up-selling.

Keep these five tips in mind as you look to strengthen your customer relationships in the coming year.

29

Don't Leave Fish to Find Fish

Last week, I went king salmon fishing on Lake Michigan. I have been an avid fisherman my entire life, but given my unfamiliarity with salmon and Lake Michigan, I chartered a guide to help me find and catch some of these amazing fish. Our captain, Mark, was a former search and rescue Coast Guard officer and regularly competed in salmon fishing tournaments. He knows the water and he knows his fish. After leaving the dock at 5AM, we were on fish by 6. However, after about an hour, the bite slowed down. The temptation to move to another spot was strong, but that's when Mark told us the number one rule of fishing: "don't ever leave fish to find fish." And herein lies so much truth for us as business owners.

We all want to grow our janitorial businesses. And when we think of growth, we always think of sales – new sales. And true enough, we need new sales to grow our business. But we can make a fatal mistake by neglecting our own fields in search of greener pastures. Statistics show that it is much cheaper to keep customers than to acquire new ones. Harvard Business Reviews says that getting new customers can be between 5 and 25 times more expensive that keeping existing ones. Additionally, increasing customer retention by just 5% can boost profits by as much as 25% according to invespcro.com.

So, let's get practical. How can you fish in the waters you already have to increase the growth and profits of your company.

Price Increases – If you are providing top notch service and your relationship is strong with the client, you should be able to get small price increases over time. These increases go straight to your bottom line.

Increasing Scope of Services – Is there the possibility of adding to the daily routine of work you currently perform? Maybe a day porter or cleaning new areas currently not cleaned?

Project Work – What extra-bill services could you add to increase revenue and profit? Floor work? Window cleaning? Spring cleaning? Painting? Carpet cleaning?

Referrals – Sometimes your best sources of new business are referrals from your existing clients. Reference letters or direct referrals to new clients can be VERY POWERFUL. Do not neglect this source.

So remember, don't leave fish to find fish. Your best sources of profit are right in your own back yard. In fact, they are your very own customers.

30

Leading Indicators: Why Profit Isn't Good Enough

As owners and leaders of our cleaning companies, we often measure the health and performance of our organization using lagging indicators. Lagging indicators are basically metrics that look back on how you performed over the last few weeks, months, or years. They are numbers that show where we are now as a result of things we've done in the past. The most common lagging indicator is our monthly profit and loss statement. After the month has closed and the financials are complete, we can look back and see how we did financially in the previous month. However, there is a problem.

Because lagging indicators tell you how you did in the past, they have almost no value in telling you how you will do in the future. Now don't get me wrong, we need to know how we performed in the past. Employee turnover, inspection scores, income statements, contract renewal rates, etc. are all important metrics to track. However, if we want to know how we are going to perform in the future and make modifications to meet goals, we need leading indicators.

Leading indicators or measures of things happening now that will predict how we will do in the future. For instance, if you want to improve employee turnover, what activities are critical to keep turnover low? Find out what these are then track them. Applicants per job posting, employee engagement, and other activities may predict your future turnover.

One more example of leading indicators that is important has to do with profit. Instead of letting your monthly P&L be the way you track performance, let daily hours reports be the mechanism with which you "predict" the future profit for that period.

Let me encourage you to assess your company and find some leading indicators that will help you achieve the lagging results you want. Here are a few categories of lagging indicators and some corresponding leading indicators.

Lagging Indicator: Monthly P&L

Leading Indicator: Daily hours budget

Lagging Indicator: Cash flow

Leading Indicator: Invoice aging

Lagging Indicator: Employee Turnover

Leading Indicator: Applicants per job opening

Leading Indicator: Percent of employees onboarded properly

Leading Indicator: Employee engagement

Lagging Indicator: Customer Retention

Leading Indicator: Net promoter scores

Leading Indicator: Proactive meetings

31

Three Signs of a Bad Customer

In an industry where margins are often thin, BSCs cannot afford to take on and keep the wrong types of clients. Bad customers suck the time, energy, and profits right out of your organization. So how can you avoid landing these sorts of clients? What warning signs should you be looking for in the sales process to notify you of trouble? Let me offer three.

Price Only Bid

When you encounter a prospect who is only concerned with price, red flags should be raised. These types of customers will not only beat you up on the front end to get your price low, but they will typically not tolerate service issues. Because they view your company as a commodity, they figure they can easily switch to another low-cost provider if things get tough with you. This creates a downward spiral of working hard to keep the customer, squeezing profit margins, and mounting pressure on you. If you find a price-only prospect that doesn't care about a long-term partnership, be on guard.

Switching contractors frequently

The next red flag to watch for is a prospect who switches vendors frequently. While this may be a symptom of a price-only mentality, it may signal a customer who is difficult to deal with. Customers that change vendors frequently don't value the cleaning company as a partner, but rather a lowly supplier. They don't value your people or you work, but view themselves as having the upper hand and willing to use it at all times. These customers aren't looking for partner vendors, so they probably aren't a good fit for you. When a customer refuses to see you as a partner, your likelihood of success is small. Don't expend too much energy with these types of customers when others are waiting for a quality company like you.

In the wrong market segment/geography

Finally, we can often be lured into bidding on jobs that just don't make sense for our company. Perhaps the customer is in a geography that is a bit far or maybe they are a type of building that is difficult to service. For instance, if you are used to serving commercial office and medical facilities in the evening, it can be difficult to take on an early morning retail location. Prospects should always be an operational fit for your management team. When you select a customer that is a bad fit, you end up expending energy on the bad fit while your core customers suffer. This is a lose-lose situation.

I completely understand that turning down business is hard, especially when you are eager to grow. But it pays to be patient and put all your energy into the right customers.

Define what the ideal prospect looks like, then say no to everything else. Remember, the riches are in the niches.

32

Should Area Managers Handle Customer Relations?

In the BSC world, a debate rages (ok, perhaps that's a bit strong) as to whether or not field managers and supervisors should be the primary point of contact for customers. Should these managers be responsible for the employees and cleaning only or should they also be responsible for client relations? There are some serious concerns that many have about a janitorial manager handling both. Can I find someone with the skillset to do both? Can a person handle customer relations during the day and cleaning at night?

If a company is going to scale up, I am convinced that we must convert our field management team to handling both supervision and customer relations. Here are three reasons.

Reason #1 - Scalability

As a cleaning operation grows, a company must find an operational model that can scale with the growth. Processes that are in place now should be able to handle a business 50% or 100% larger than your current size. Additionally, simplicity makes scalability easier. So the simpler your management model, the easier it is to grow and handle that growth. If every new customer required two managers (one for supervision and one for client relations), then your operation is complicated and makes growth more difficult to handle. Remember, simplicity is key!

Reason #2 – Cost Control

If every account requires two managers to run the job (one for supervision and one for client relations), you are likely increasing the overhead necessary to run your cleaning business. At my company, we switched from a "two manager model" to a "single manager model" and saved approximately $30k/yr at one of our branches. When you create savings like these, you can then afford to pay higher wages or offer better incentives, a true win-win.

Reason #3 – Ownership

The final, and perhaps most important reason for switching to a single manager model is that it creates an ownership mentality among your management team. When we had supervisors who were only responsible for the evening cleaning work, but not the customer relations, the supervisors were focused primary on getting the accounts staffed and cleaned. There was no real awareness of what the customer wanted because they never interacted with the customer. Therefore, they never really "owned" the account in a holistic sense. But once managers started meeting with clients and learned their expectations, it began to shape how they supervised the evening cleaning work. This helped with quality and customer retention.

So, my challenge to you is this: assess your current operational model and ask yourself the following questions.

- Is my operation scalable with my current management structure?
- Is my management structure cost effective?
- Does my current management model create an ownership mentality among my supervisory team?

33

Profit Sharing With Managers

Recently I had a conversation with a coaching client of mine about how he can find efficiencies on a new, large account he just landed. His company is around $1 million in revenue and this new client will nearly double the size of his business. And even better, it is a five-year contract. However, the margins are a little tighter than he'd like and he wants to improve those year over year. We discussed equipment efficiencies, labor reduction strategies, etc. However, there is one strategy that stands head and shoulders above the rest - one move you can make to promote long-term expense reduction. And the answer is...*profit sharing with your project manager.*

Most project managers have one primary objective, making sure the customer is happy. Second in line is the budget. As long as they are within budget and the customer is happy, all is well. However, with nothing but a base salary, there is little incentive to reduce job expenses. In fact, what would motivate a manager to accomplish the same job with less people if that could make it more difficult to keep the customer happy?

The answer lies in profit sharing. Imagine a$30k/month job that is operating on a 20% profit margin ($6k/month). Instead of fighting with the manager to convince him/her to reduce hours, what if you offered 1/3 of every dollar you made above goal in the form of a bonus? If you beat the profit goal by $600, they would get a $200 bonus. If you beat it by $1,200, they would get a $400 bonus. This keeps the owner from being the budget nazi, always harassing the manager to cut expenses, and uses positive reinforcement to get the results you want. In addition to reducing tension, this helps cultivate an ownership mentality among your management team, a true WIN-WIN.

My only recommendation is to tie the bonus to customer satisfaction so that the manager doesn't jeopardize the account in pursuit of a bonus. For instance, customer satisfaction must be at least a 7/10 for the manager to be eligible for profit sharing.

For those of you that are hesitant to share profits, you must be willing to let go. When people are treated like owners, they will act like owners, and everyone wins. Give it a try! I promise it will work if done correctly.

34

Three Important Questions about Add Services

In an industry where few companies can break past a profit margin of 10%, most janitorial contractors are easily enticed by the opportunity of higher margin work. We are always looking for that next golden opportunity to help boost our margins. But given the countless different ways you can earn extra revenue in your BSC business, how do you decide which opportunities to pursue? How do you know which add-services are good and which ones are not? Let me offer a quick guide.

First, a distinction needs to be made. An add-service is something extra you provide your customers in addition to your core service. An example would be carpet cleaning. A separate business unit, on the other hand, is a service that has its own unique customer base and operational model. For all intents and purposes, it is a different business altogether.

Residential carpet cleaning or remodeling would be an example. In this article, I am talking about add-services.

Here are the criteria you should use to determine whether or not a particular add-service is right for you.

Does it complement your core service?

Imagine that your bank also offered oil-changing services. This sounds incredibly bizarre because it is not remotely related to professional banking services. In fact, it would hurt the professional image the bank had. In similar fashion, a BSC must be careful to only add services that complement the core service. If the add-service is not complementary, it could decrease your perceived value. If you fail at the service, your cleaning operation could be in jeopardy. Likewise, if the add-service is so different from the cleaning service, the customer may not see it as adding value. Add-services should ALWAYS complement and strengthen the core, but NEVER detract from it.

Does it give synergy to your operation?

Some add-services may complement your core janitorial service, but because of their difficulty to implement, they could become a drain on your operation. For instance, recycle programs may complement your cleaning operation, but the time and energy needed to successfully run a recycle program could weaken your core operation. Every company has different strengths and weaknesses, and some services may add operational synergy to one company while reducing synergy at another.

Is it profitable?

While an add-service may complement your core service and give synergy to your operation, if it is not profitable, you should not pursue it. There was a time when my company did not have the purchasing power to resell supplies at a healthy margin. While this add-service would be complementary and give us synergy, it was not profitable at the time. Therefore, it did not make sense to offer it to customers. Make sure that all of your add-services are profiting at least 30% (with the exception of supply resale). If you can't get 30%, find another service.

35

Contracts to Protect Yourself

There are generally two responses you hear from janitorial contractors when asked their opinion on contracts with customers. Some people think contracts don't matter. They say that when a customer wants to sever the relationship, there is nothing you can do. Others take a very contract-centered approach, assuming the account is only as secure as the terms of the contract. Well, there is certainly some truth in both approaches. When a customer wants out, they usually find a way to get out. Likewise, when they are being really well served, the terms of the agreement rarely matter.

But despite good intentions by both contractor and customer, there will inevitably come a time when good contract terms will be needed to shield both parties from harm. In my mind, there is no clause more important for the contractor than a well-written term/termination clause.

In the past, most janitorial contracts had termination clauses that required the customer or contractor to give the other party a 30-day notice before terminating the agreement. Other than this written thirty-day notice, no other reason was needed. This essentially reduced every contract to a 30-day agreement, even if the term stated it was three or five years. When a customer can cancel at any time, there truly is no contract term.

To combat this situation, contractors need a robust termination clause that protects both the contractor and the customer. While I am not an attorney and this is not legal advice, I would recommend having a termination clause similar to this one.

Sample Term-Termination Clause
This Agreement shall remain in effect for a period of _____ years, with the term of service commencing on __________ and ending on ____________. This Agreement will automatically renew for additional one-year terms upon the same terms and conditions, unless either party to this Agreement provides written notice of its desire to terminate this Agreement within 60 days of the end of the then-current term or renewal term. Termination of this Agreement prior to expiration of the term can only be predicated on uncorrected service issues within the scope of services, as set forth herein. Prior to cancellation of services by the Client, Contractor must be notified in detail in writing of the issue and provided not less than fifteen (15) days to correct the issue. If the issue is not resolved, Client shall provide a 30-day written notice of cancellation before terminating the Agreement.

This contract clause protects the contractor from willy-nilly cancellations; however, it protects the customer from being stuck with subpar service. While we rarely would pursue legal action over a contract cancellation, this clause usually prevents those situations from ever arising.

In closing, I would recommend you speak with your attorney and consider a term/termination clause similar to the one above. Agreements should always be fair and protect both parties, and I am convinced the above terms help make that possible.

36

How To Reduce Your Labor Expense

Labor Savings Tip #1 – Mobile or Telephone Timekeeping
Managing labor is the name of the game in the janitorial industry. 60%+ of our expenses are tied directly to labor. If you can properly manage this labor, you will maximize your profit potential.

The first step to managing labor is accurately tracking how much labor is being spent on each job. Prior to the onset of the tech revolution, most companies used timecards that were either filled out manually or punched via a time clock on the job. In the janitorial industry, time clocks were not often present, so workers were on the honor system to fill out their timecards accurately.

Even giving most workers the benefit of the doubt, rounding up and a few deceitful employees could impact your nightly hours by a decent amount. Just two hours per night of "false time" would cost a company about $6,000 over the course of the year. This is no small amount.

To limit the amount of "false time," every janitorial contractor should make full use of electronic timekeeping. Many systems are available that require employees to clock in via a landline or mobile device (tracking the location), to ensure time recorded is actually being spent on the job. For every employee that saves 10 minutes per night, this equates to over $500/yr in savings.

Labor Savings Tip #2 – Timekeeping Reports & Budgets

While tip number one helps you reduce "false time" and maximize labor accuracy, tip number two focuses on managing those hours actually being worked. Nearly every mobile or telephone timekeeping system generates labor data that can be tracked daily. Each day, managers should review reports of the previous day's labor, broken down by job. Each job should have budget hours that you compare actual hours to.

For instance, if a job is budgeted for 6 hours per night, you want to ensure the hours being worked consistently stay at or below six hours per night. If you don't monitor these hours on a daily basis, you can't make corrections before it's too late and you've lost money. The goal of daily hours reviews is to ensure labor doesn't go over budget, while at the same time workers aren't neglecting an account, leading to a quality issue.

One additional benefit of hours reports is being able to compare labor hours across jobs, looking for potential efficiencies. If two facilities of similar size and density are cleaned at different rates, this should indicate a potential labor savings at the less efficient account.

Labor Savings Tip #3 – Watching For Exact Hour Amounts

Imagine this scenario: you have an employee who is working at a building and they are logging exactly six hours per night. What is potentially going on in this situation? It is very possible that the employee has in his/her mind that they are allotted a certain amount of time and they intend to get paid for that amount of time each night. As a wise manager once said, "Work expands to fill the time you give it." One of the advantages of a mobile or telephone timekeeping system is to pay only for the hours worked. So when you see exact hours being worked on a consistent basis, likely an employee is working less than the amount recorded.

Now to be fair to our hardworking people, I don't want to encourage you to beat them up and unnecessarily cut their hours. Many of our workers are under-appreciated and need our support and encouragement. However, we also can't afford to pay for unnecessary hours. Be fair, treat your people with dignity, but don't allow hours to be wasted.

Labor Savings Tip #4 - Holiday Savings Plan

With labor accounting for roughly 60% of total costs, any chance to save labor will be a chance to increase profits. And major holidays are a perfect place to make that happen. When you consider the main holidays that often fall on weekdays (Christmas, Thanksgiving, Labor Day, Memorial Day, New Year's Day, and Independence Day), you find six opportunities to save on labor. However, this goes beyond saving money on the holiday alone.

Most every customer you serve observes these six holidays and allows their employees time off during them. Likewise, they rarely expect cleaning on these days. However, many companies are flexible with their employees on the day before major holidays, giving them the opportunity to leave early. Knowing their expectations can be lower on these holiday eves, contractors can coordinate with their customer contacts to inquire about a one-time limited service scope. Such a limited scope could include such things as spot vacuuming traffic areas as opposed to full vacuums, spot mopping instead of full mops, etc.

Let's do a simple calculation to show how the types of saving you can gain. Assume a janitorial contractor has about 200 labor hours each evening and could save 25% with a holiday savings plan. With six holidays per year and $12/hr per employee, this would equate to an annual savings of $3,600.

Implement these labor-saving tips, and you *will* save money!

37

Keep Supply Expense Below 2.5%

Outside of labor, janitorial supplies are the greatest job cost expense contractors have to control. For years, my company struggled to keep our supply expenses in line. We were typically above 4% (as a percent of revenue) and sometimes flirted with the 5% number. However, over the last few years, we implemented several changes that have kept our supply expense below 2.5% month after month. For a company the size of mine (approx. $19M), this is an annual savings of $270,000. Here are the four specific things we did to make this happen.

#1 - Streamline Products

A prime cause of supply overspend is buying too many products, specifically ones you don't really need. When you don't have parameters on what you intend to use on every job, everything becomes an option – supply creep sets in. As I look back to our supply list 10 years ago, we had special dusting rags, stainless steel cleaner, magic eraser pads, upright vacuums, detail vacuums, and on and on. Now our supplies list is much shorter, saving valuable money on each job without sacrificing quality. The simple fact is that more supply options don't necessarily improve cleaning quality (at least in the eyes of the customer).

#2 - Dispensing Systems

This is a big money saver. Ready to use chemicals are MUCH more expensive (per bottle) than chemicals dispensed using a chemical concentrate dispensing system. The savings per bottle can range from 50% to 90%. For those unfamiliar, dispensing stations are simply wall-mounted units that mix water and chemical concentrates to give you ready to use chemical. The station automatically handles the dilution ratio so you get the same concentration each time. This cuts down on inventory space, bottle waste (as you can reuse bottles), and most importantly, expenses. For those accounts that don't have room for a chemical dispensing station, just install one at the home office and refill bottles as needed.

If you want to save money fast, switch to a dispensing station NOW. Nearly every major chemical manufacturer has one to offer.

#3 - Supplier Delivery

Several years ago, we had supply "cages" at each of our office locations. This was basically a room or caged-off area where we kept supplies. Managers would check out products from this supply cage, take it to the jobsite, then admin would record the expense to the appropriate job. When inventory ran low, admin would place an order to replenish. For those versed in LEAN manufacturing principles, let's just say "we had some waste in the system."

After looking at our process and becoming frustrated with the amount of supply delivery our managers were doing, we decided to push all supply delivery onto our distributors. Since we were already placing orders with our distributor, we decided to schedule a weekly order and arrange for them to drop ship the items to the appropriate job site. The biggest savings here was keeping our managers focused on managing jobs instead of distributing supplies.

#4 - Buying Group Member

Our final push to save money on supplies was joining an industry buying group, the National Service Alliance (NSA). The NSA accepts members who have at least $2M in revenue, giving them access to the purchasing power of national contractors. Now if you aren't quite at the $2M mark, don't worry. Programs like BSCAI's Purchase Advantage Program give contractors access to good pricing and discounts. While they may not be quite as good as the NSA discounts, the pricing is still better than what you can do on your own.

Conclusion

In an industry where margins are already tight, increasing profits by 1% of revenue is significant – a 20% increase for a company with a 5% net margin. Supply savings are low hanging fruit to be added to your bottom line. All the suggestions mentioned above are easy to implement and a byproduct will be increased time spent managing accounts. Don't miss out!

38

How to Increase Manager Compensation and Profit

In my opinion, field managers in the janitorial industry have the hardest job. First, they must manage relationships with clients, deal with complaints, requests, and other issues. Second, they must manage their workforce, often hiring, training, and ensuring all jobs are filled each day. This can be a grueling task, even for the best of managers.

While this job is the hardest job (one I don't envy), it is also one of the most important roles in any company. This manager is usually the face of the company in the eyes of the customer. However, most BSC field managers don't make extravagant salaries, nor can owners afford to pay them such. A typical salary for a field manager is between $30k and $50k per year, depending upon the workload, area of the country, and other factors.

You want to attract and retain high caliber managers at your commercial cleaning business. You want to offer them competitive wages, but you feel your profit margins only allow you to pay so much. I've got a solution! Let me offer three creative ways you can provide extra compensation for your managers while simultaneously boosting company profit.

Compensation Option #1 – Extra Bill Commission

Extra bill work (hard floor care, carpet cleaning, window washing, etc.) is usually very profitable, with margins often exceeding 50%. However, managers are often leery of pursuing such work as it typically increases their workload. However, if you offer managers a sales commission (or profit sharing) on extra bill work, their reluctance will likely turn to eagerness. At my company, we offer 10% - 15% profit sharing on all extra-bill work with a goal of 7% gross revenue coming from extra-bill projects. So, if a manager is overseeing $50k in monthly revenue and acquires 7% of that in special projects at 50% profit margin, they could make an additional $250/month or $3,000 per year. For a manager making $40k per year, this is a 7.5% pay increase. For the company, this is an $18,000 increase in annual profit. This is a true win/win!

Compensation Option #2 – Finder's Fees

Our company is always looking for new customers that fit our ideal client profile. However, identifying these potentials and getting our foot in the door can be a real challenge. Field managers can be a big help here. Since they are out visiting accounts on a regular basis, they drive past potential clients every night. Additionally, they interact with facility managers who talk with other facility managers. If our area or project managers can help us land a new account, we allow them to share in a portion of the sales commissions. The larger and more profitable the account, the greater their payout.

Compensation Option #3 – Branch Boards

This last method of additional compensation is probably the most lucrative (for both the company and the manager) and influential of all the options we have explored in the past. This idea was shared with me by a fellow consultant, Dana Weaver. Branch boards work like this. Each operational unit of the organization (which may be just one if you are a small company), is given a profit goal to hit for the year. For every dollar the branch/unit achieves above and beyond that goal, we share a significant percentage with them (40% is our number). The company wins because we only expected the "goal" amount. Everything above is "icing on the cake" for the company. However, the managers win big because they get to share in those profits. At my company, we divvy up the 40% among the key managers. This incentive program really gets the managers motivated to increase profit by lowering labor costs, renewing contracts, keeping supply costs low, etc.

The Key to Good Compensation Plans

Regardless of the additional compensation plans you offer, let me make a suggestion. Make sure the plan (whatever it is) drives the behavior you wish to promote. If you don't want to land 2x per week accounts, then don't pay commission on them. If you don't want strip and wax work, then don't pay commission on it. Incentivize the achievement of outcomes best for the company. This aligns manager interests with company interests, creating a true WIN/WIN.

39

Reports Your Managers Need

Management (in any industry) is the art of getting things done through the coordination and oversight of multiple people, products, and processes. But in order for a manager to do their job effectively, they need information to help them make decisions. The cleaning industry is no different. The managers who oversee your daily cleaning operations need certain accurate and timely information to do their jobs well. Without this information they are left to manage and make decisions in the dark.

While getting out, visiting accounts, and interacting with the team members is certainly necessary, it is impossible for a manager to be everywhere at once. This is where reports can become very valuable in knowing without being present. For area, project, and operations managers, three reports are key to getting a complete picture of the happenings on the jobs.

Daily Hours Budget Report

The daily hours budget report is perhaps the single most important of the three reports because it gives daily information about the jobs. This report is basically a summary of the hours worked by each employee broken down by job. So, for instance, if you manage ABC Bank, you can see who worked there last night and how many hours they worked. Additionally, if budgets are set up correctly, you can constantly compare the hours worked to the hours budgeted.

This report gives your managers two distinct advantages. First, it helps them monitor quality by ensuring that ample time is spent at each account each night. A sure indicator of quality problems is a steady reduction of cleaning hours. You can stay ahead of quality problems by monitoring hours daily and catching problems before they balloon. Second, the daily hours budget report helps your managers ensure jobs are always profiting as planned. With labor accounting for about 60% of all costs, monitoring hours is the driver of company profitability. When this is done effectively on a micro level, you can ensure that profits will occur on a macro level. It makes for a truly scalable model.

Monthly Job Cost Statement

This report zooms out the lens on the jobs and looks at a monthly snapshot of the account. It is basically a profit and loss statement broken down by job. At my company, managers get a monthly statement for their accounts. With each account, they can track labor dollars, supply costs, overtime expense, and more. This allows our managers to be mini-business owners, taking charge of their piece of the company. Each month, they identify poorly performing accounts and put plans in place to get the accounts back on track. Once again, these reports give a micro-level summary of different parts of the business. If each manager is managing the accounts appropriately, we can expect consistent profitability, all other things being equal.

Monthly Branch/Company P&L

I am a huge fan of open book management. Exposing your company financials helps build trust among your management team while also cultivating ownership at all levels of the organization. I would encourage you not to be reluctant here. If you have things to hide from your team members, then you probably are doing something you shouldn't be doing. I have found that open books keep me accountable, which is a great check and balance on leadership.

Monthly profit and loss statements help your managers see how their group of accounts ties into the branch as a whole. When they are disconnected from this information, you should expect decisions in keeping with a disconnected attitude or mentality. While this is a topic for another day, I would also encourage you to compensate your managers based upon both account performance and overall branch performance. If you want team players, you must treat them as part of the team.

How Can I Get These Reports

If you are a smaller contractor without a lot of fancy technology you may be asking, "How can I get these reports?"

Well, it is actually easier than what you think. For the budget hours report, you can use one of the many mobile timekeeping systems available. There are some specific to the janitorial industry (e.g. Swept) and there are others that are more universal in nature. For the other two reports, QuickBooks or any other reputable accounting software should do the trick. For those of you larger firms (100 or more employees), I would recommend an industry specific all-in-one solution such as TEAM (which my company uses) or MITC. I can literally print these reports in less than two minutes.

However, the key is more about the data input than the specific program you use. If you are not accurately inputting employee time and other costs, then you cannot expect to get accurate reports. Garbage in, garbage out.

If you aren't using these reports yet, then don't wait. I promise it will help you and your managers make better decisions.

40

Getting a Price Increase

Asking for a price increase from one of your customers can be one of the most challenging and intimidating tasks for any manager. While this seems to be par for the course in many industries, janitorial contractors often struggle with this aspect. There are many reasons for this. Some people are just plain afraid of conflict – they'd rather not wake the sleeping dog. Others are afraid that asking for a price increase will invoke the customer to get other bids. Still others assume that since we are a complaint driven industry, the customer will not be receptive to any sort of price increase without a long history of remarkably stellar service.

Despite our fear or trepidation to go after price increases, WE MUST! We leave money on the table, squeeze profits out of the business, and interestingly enough, we don't do what most customers already expect from us. So, to help you gain confidence in asking for an increase, let me lay out a 5-step plan you can implement to get those increases.

Remember, price increases add profit directly to the bottom line. You can't afford not to get them.

Step 1 – Know Your Job

Before you approach your customer about a price increase, you must have a complete understanding of the status of your job. At a bare minimum, you need a good grip on the following information:

- Are the specifications you bid the same specifications you are carrying out currently?
- Did you have a consistently healthy profit margin spanning the last six months? How did this compare to what you initially bid? Are labor hours and supply costs close to your initial estimate? If you are not doing an accurate job cost statement each month, then you cannot accurately answer this question.

Without this information, you don't have the foundational knowledge needed to justify your price increase. A price increase always requires justification, and knowing your job gives you part of the information needed to make your pitch.

Step 2 – Know Your Customer

Having a thorough grasp on your job is the first half of the foundational equation. The other half is knowing your customers. You may know your job, profit margin, costs, etc., but without knowing the status of the relationship with your customer, you are not in a solid position to negotiate for a price increase. Here are the basics you need to know.

How does the customer feel about the level of your service? Have you been doing regular (i.e. monthly) partnership meetings and getting an overall score from your customer contact. Six months of scores averaging 8/10 or higher means the service and satisfaction level is high. Without a good gauge of your service level (from the customer's perspective), you are not in a good position to negotiate for an increase.

How does the customer feel about the relationship? There is a difference between great levels of service and a great relationship. Many cleaning contracts have been lost despite great service. If communication has been strong in addition to great service scores, you are ready to move to step 3.

Step 3 – Recap the Big Picture

Anytime you deliver information that may be difficult to swallow, always begin with a recap of your relationship. In step 3, your goal is to help the customer see a couple of things. First, due to the complaint-driven nature of our industry, you need to reinforce your value to the customer. Explain to them the progress you have made, share with them the great quality scores, and let them know the value you add. Second, communicate your desire to form a long-term partnership. I like this word "partnership" because it sends the message of a mutually beneficial relationship. When a customer believes you want to serve them well for a long-time to come, they are less likely to think of you as a cash-sucking vendor only out for a quick buck. Preach partnerships!

Step 4 – State Your Case with Honesty

As grandma said, "Honesty is the best policy." I am not an advocate of pretending that margins are tight when they are not or complaining that costs have risen when in fact they have not. If your bluff is called, then credibility and trust are gone forever. Instead, be honest with your customer. You want to serve them well and make a fair profit. Now explain to them the obstacles to making that happen. Here are a few potential reasons:

You mis bid the job. Let's face it, this happens sometimes. When it does, it is usually best to stick it out for a while, then go after your price increase at renewal time. Don't be afraid to admit this mistake. If the customer wants you to succeed in your service, they will understand that you can't continue at the same service level for the same price.

The scope has changed. Scope creep is a very common thing in service contracts. Small tasks get added over time that add up to significant hours each month. By knowing your specs and the additional scope items, you can easily make your case for the increase.

The expectations have changed or were misjudged. "Clean" is an ever-moving target, a subjective expectation that varies from customer to customer. Part of bidding is judging the "clean-factor." There are times when we flat miss the expectation level and need to ramp up hours to meet customer demands. This can be the hardest reason to convince a customer of a needed increase, but if communication has been solid, you should be able to get on the same page.

Cleaners need a raise. If the customer has quality as a top priority or they really like some of your staff, then they will understand that cleaner pay rate matters. Make sure to add more than the actual pay increase to cover taxes, profit, and additional future pay increases.

Other costs have risen. The last few years have given rise to external factors increasing our costs of doing business, with health insurance and minimum wage hikes being the two major ones. These and other external cost drivers are easy to explain and usually don't come with much pushback.

During this step, let me encourage you to be open about your job costs. I don't recommend getting overly specific but be "sufficiently vague", so they understand how the costs are derived. When the customer understands how your costs are figured, they will be in a better position to sympathize with your case.

Step 5 – Ask Them "Do You Think This Is Fair?"

I absolutely love this question! If they answer with "Yes," then they have agreed to your case. If they answer no, then they are in a position to explain why what you said is not fair. If you have been honest in your reasoning, then this is a tough task for the customer. To say your case is unfair implies that you have been dishonest or are asking for something unreasonable. Now they are in the hot seat to explain why.

The most difficult response to deal with will be a customer who acknowledges your case is fair but says they don't have the budget to make it happen. In this case, your response should be, "Well, Mr. Customer, what things could we eliminate from our current scope of service to make up for these additional costs I have incurred so that we can keep service quality at a level you expect?" Once again, you have placed them in the driver's seat of answering the hard questions.

Bonus #1 – Update Contracts

One of the great things about price increases or price changes is they give you the opportunity to update your contract and lengthen your term of agreement. Anytime you get a price increase, *always* sign an updated contract with newer and longer terms of service.

Bonus #2 – Give Price Reductions

If you want to forever solidify your relationship with a customer, give them a small price reduction. Trust is built when another person believes you have their best interests at heart. When you offer a price reduction, you can be sure that trust will grow, and the threat of rebidding will be nearly eliminated. The two situations that make price reductions possible are as follows: (1) You have a profit margin that is higher than what you normally expect out of an account. (2) You offer some scope reductions that don't affect perceived quality.

Bonus #3 – Add Additional Services

Adding additional services is a great way to skirt the "price increase" conversation. If you think a customer could use an additional service you offer, you can often wrap up your needed increase into that extra service, or at least lower the needed increase. This can help ensure the customer feels well taken care of.

Your 30-Day Challenge

I want to encourage you to go get a price increase over the next 30 days. If you are not accustomed to getting increases, start with a small customer. Doing hard things will become easier with practice. If you use the above steps and you find success, let me know. I want to hear your story!

Human Resources

41

Recruiting Cleaners with Facebook

When I mention Facebook, you may be tempted to think of political rants, pictures of people pretending to have a perfect life, or workout selfies. And true enough, there are more of those things in my Facebook feed than I care to see. However, Facebook can be a remarkably powerful recruiting tool for you and your cleaning business. And in an industry where staffing ranks as one of the chief struggles, you cannot afford to neglect this audience of 240+ million people. I want to offer you three ways you can recruit cleaners on Facebook.

Before I offer these three tips, you need to set up a Facebook business page. This is a simple and free process.

Facebook Recruiting Tip #1

My first and favorite way to recruit on Facebook is by creating ads on my business page. You can do this by going to your campaign manager and creating an ad or by simply posting a help wanted post on your business page wall and then "boosting" that post. For just $20-$40, you can cause your post to show up in front of several thousand people matching whatever demographic information you select. Facebook lets you target by age, geography, income, and a host of other factors. If your ad looks halfway decent, you can get click on your job ad for $0.20-$0.50.

Facebook Recruiting Tip #2

Facebook recently came out with their own job search platform. This new feature allows you to post a job from your business page, specifying the job type, pay, and location. This will allow job seekers in your targeted area to see your job openings. Applicants can then apply right on Facebook. The downside to this feature is that it doesn't allow you to redirect applicants to your website.

Facebook Recruiting Tip #3

The final Facebook tip is to use Facebook groups to post your job ads. Nearly every town or county has multiple Facebook groups dedicated to buying, selling, and even jobs. These can be both public and private groups and often contain tens of thousands of users. If you combine this tip along with the other two, you can reach thousands of people for less than a new pair of shoes.

Recruiting doesn't have to be a budget breaker and Facebook makes that possible. Give it a try.

42

They Accused My Cleaner of Stealing

The cleaning staff will forever be the scapegoat for things gone wrong, especially when something turns up missing. Like it or not, this is the situation we find ourselves in. Every facility we clean is full of people: employees, guests, contractors, and more. But when something goes missing, the customer usually assumes it didn't happen under their watch. Rather, it must have happened at night when the cleaning crew was there. And let's face it, this is probably the assumption we would make as well.

So, you get that dreaded phone call. "Jordan, this is Jim from ABC manufacturing. We had an iPad go missing from the HR office and your cleaners were the only people here last night. It must have been them. I don't see how it could possibly be anyone else. We need to talk."

How do we handle this situation? We feel pinned against the wall and may even feel a twinge of guilt, even though no proof has been levied against us – only circumstantial evidence at best. Well, let me offer 3 simple steps to help you walk through every theft accusation.

Step 1 – Don't assume guilt

Your cleaner may have taken the item in question, but they may not. You don't know. So don't *ever* assume that your company (and your employee) is guilty just because you've been accused. We want to stand by our team, support them, and give them the benefit of the doubt. This does not mean we deny being involved; rather, we just listen and understand what the customer is saying. So, for instance, after being accused, you may respond like this: "Mr. Customer, I'm very sorry this has happened. It sounds very frustrating. What can I do to help you get this resolved?" By being sympathetic and helpful, you aren't assuming guilt nor are you being combative.

Step 2 – Commit to doing the right thing

Next, you want to commit to doing what is right to get the situation resolved. This will involve a few things:

- Ask the customer how you can help resolve the issue.
- Commit to doing an internal investigation.
- Cooperate with the customer's own investigation.

Your goal here is to be a seeker of truth and justice. I know that sounds pie in the sky, but it should be true. Business leaders should be men and women of integrity, committed to doing what is right.

Step 3 – Follow up and follow through

Finally, you want to follow up with the customer on your findings and follow through with any reparations (if needed). If you find out that you are guilty, confess and commit to paying back what needs to be paid back. However, if you are not convinced that your team is guilty, be honest with the customer about your findings. Paying something you don't owe to relieve the tension is the coward's way out. If they are convinced of your guilt, but you aren't, perhaps be willing to move the employee in question to a new site as a means of compromise. Never admit to guilt that isn't yours to own.

Our commitment to our people and our customers will often put us in tough spots. Balancing the needs of these two parties can create tension in our organization, but compromise can be the remedy. So, keep these three principles in mind as you navigate the next tough situation at your company. (1) Do everything with integrity. (2) Be a loyal advocate to your employees. (3) Serve your customer with excellence.

43

Seven Interviewing Mistakes

In case you haven't already figured it out yet, getting the right people on your team is the number one challenge you face. Systems, processes, and management are easy if you have the right people. As someone once said, "Management is easy, except for the people part."

While many of us in the cleaning industry spend much time recruiting and hiring staff for our companies, rarely do we go about this endeavor with any sort of rigorous framework. We haphazardly recruit when an opening arises, then we haphazardly interview, relying on our off-the-cuff methods. While spelling out a comprehensive hiring process would take an entire book (and I have a great one to recommend below), let me point out 8 interviewing mistakes many of us make when hiring cleaners and managers.

Mistake #1 – They Have Industry Experience

I have had more hiring flops with cleaning or janitorial management backgrounds than any other. In fact, over the years

I've come to see industry experience as a strike against an applicant. Industry skills and knowledge can be learned in a relatively short period of time, whereas the more critical character traits such as humble, hungry, and smart (See Patrick Lencioni's "The Ideal Team Player") are rarely learned *at all.* As a consultant once told me, "I'd rather take a manager and make him a cleaner, than take a cleaner and try to make him a manager." Don't *ever* hire someone solely because of industry experience. It may make sense in the short run, but it will almost never be a long-term solution.

Mistake #2 – The Gut Feeling

Gut feels can work for some things in life. In fact, my wife has often been proved right about certain character assessments solely based on gut feel. But hiring is not the place for decisions based upon gut feelings. When solid data is possible to obtain, only a fool would rely on a gut feel. You need facts, examples, proof, and rigorous analysis, not feelings. As Geoff Smart says in Who, The A Method of Hiring, "If you rely on a gut feeling, you will end up with a stomachache."

Mistake #3 – Many Interviewers Equals Comprehensive Assessment

Many business owners or managers assume that having multiple people interview the same person will result in a comprehensive assessment of the interviewee. But nothing could be further from the truth. Without a strategic hiring plan, multiple interviews with different people within the company end up being multiple people asking the same shallow questions. These multiple interviews often produce multiple gut feelings.

Mistake #4 – The Suitor

Rather than probing a candidate's background for the information you need to make an informed decision, the suitor spends most of the time trying to sell the candidate on the company. The suitor assumes the candidate's qualifications and oddly turns the tables of the interview, acting as if the company is the one being interviewed. While it is important to sell the company to the right candidate, this is done much later in the hiring process.

Mistake #5 – Trying to Trick The Candidate

Have you ever thrown a piece of trash on the ground to see if the candidate would pick it up sometime during the interview? Have you ever put the interviewee under some strange test to see how they would respond? Often, we believe these hidden tests will somehow uncover some character trait we wouldn't be able to find otherwise. But once again, there is nothing scientific or systematic about such a test. So don't do it!

Mistake #6 – Making Friends

"So, you're from Kansas? That's great! My mom is from Kansas…." Many interviewers assume that making a personal connection is the sole purpose of the interview. They work hard to make this connection and then when such a connection occurs, they hire based on "feeling good" about the person. But a rigorous interview process is not about making friends; it is about finding the relevant data to make an informed decision.

Mistake #7 – What Would You Do Questions

This is perhaps the most common mistake of all, and I confess, I've used it more times than I care to admit. But asking someone "what they would do" in such and such a situation is no predictor of what they would actually do. We can all talk a good talk, especially if we know what the interviewer is looking for. But talk and action are two totally different things. Past actions are the best predictor of future actions, not talk of what one *would* do.

So what mistakes are you making now? I would encourage you to revisit your hiring process and systematize it. Ensure that every step of the process is necessary and aimed at getting the information you need to make an informed hiring decision. Remember, facts and history, not feelings and intentions, are what we need.

44

Why Donald Trump Would Make a Bad Manager

Love him or hate him, there has perhaps never been a president more polarizing than Donald Trump. His hatred of the media, willingness to say (literally) anything, and an ego the size of Texas win him both praise and disdain. While I'm a conservative who is NOT a big fan of Trump, I understand why many like him and I understand why many despise him. I get that.

However, the current political landscape can be very instructive for BSC leaders despite our political persuasion. Love it or hate it, Donald Trump is best known for his ego. I would argue that ultimately, for better or worse, this is what got him elected president. While history has yet to decide if the Trump presidency was a success, we must ask ourselves a question: "Is a Donald Trump leadership style good for our business?"

Let me pose the question another way. Would you hire a manager on your staff who had the ego of our past president? Is the ego that gets a man elected president beneficial in running a cleaning operation? For me the answer is "absolutely not!"

The janitorial industry is a servant-oriented industry. Team members are asked to perform a task most wouldn't do for a pay most wouldn't accept. Janitorial managers not only must lead and inspire these workers toward excellence but must serve company customers as well. Leading such a team will require an incredible amount of humility, service, and dedication. You must be able to take criticism and blame even when you aren't at fault. Mangers must transfer praise to their team, not seek it for themselves. Finally, they must be willing to perform the lowest of tasks alongside their workers, showing they are not too good to clean.

While I don't mean to pick on previous president, I am convinced that his sort of bravado spells disaster for leaders in our industry. We need men and women who will lead with conviction and humility - managers who put themselves last and others first. We need servant leaders who can connect with rich and poor, black and white, male and female. We need leaders of integrity.

At my company, we are looking for managers we describe as "blue collar professionals." These are men and women who know the value of hard work and professionalism, yet possess the values of humility, integrity, and excellence.

So, remember, what can get you elected as president of the most powerful country on earth can make you a terrible janitorial manager. Servant leadership is the best road to lasting success.

45

Four Traits of A+ Caliber Managers

The biggest problem you have in your cleaning company is not getting the right customers, developing the right systems, or even hiring the right cleaners. Yeah, I said it! Hiring cleaners is not your biggest obstacle. Sure, hiring cleaners may take the most time and energy, and may cause the most headaches. But front-line managers (e.g. area managers, operations managers, project managers, etc.) are the most important focus of small and mid-sized janitorial contractors.

Why is this the case? First, these managers are most often responsible for hiring the end cleaners. Second, they are responsible for implementing company systems and ensuring that all work is carried out as promised to the customer. Finally, these managers typically maintain the personal relationships with the customers. Without high-level managers, your company will be mediocre at best, have no chance of real growth, and the owner will never find true freedom.

Finding A+ talent can be difficult. I certainly have hired my share of bad apples. And while there are many tried and true steps in a successful hiring process, one of the very first is identifying the key traits or attributes needed in your managers. Over the years, we have identified four primary characteristics that seem to be associated with A-Level managers. (The first three traits are found in Patrick Lincioni's "The Ideal Team Player.")

#1 – Humble

Great leaders are humble, and two of the best business books of all time (Good to Great and The Bible) make this clear. Humility is not some self-effacing, woe is me attitude that allows people to walk all over you. Rather, humility results in a quiet confidence that doesn't need to boast or be recognized. As C.S Lewis once said, "Humility is not thinking less of yourself, but thinking of yourself less." Humble leaders are able to put the needs of the company and others above their own. Such an attitude wins the affection of followers and ensures higher output. A leader who lacks humility is certain to have difficulty running a large crew of people doing a job that most wouldn't do for pay that many find undesirable.

Another reason humility is so important has to do with the nature of our industry. Let's face it, the janitorial industry is not sexy or glamorous. Any manager who feels "too good" to do the actual work *will never* be able to motivate a team of people to perform that work. Conviction can't be faked, and if workers sniff a hint of arrogance, morale and motivation are out the window. If cleaning a toilet is beneath a manager, then he /she is unworthy of the job.

#2 – Hungry

Your front-line managers (and in fact, all of your company leaders) need to be hungry. By hungry I mean motivated, competitive, and determined to succeed. You do not want managers who are looking for a J-O-B. If someone just wants to come to work, put in their hours and go home, then they are not a good fit. Hungry leaders are always looking for an edge, looking for ways to get better and better. They want to win. They want to be the best, proving to the customer and you that they are the right fit. Hungry managers aren't satisfied with the status quo – they want to grow the company and grow their career. What is particularly interesting about hungry people is that while money is certainly a driver, humble and hungry leaders are more concerned with the challenge and accomplishment then they are the money. A team of hungry players will not need you constantly driving them to achieve the goal. They just need a goal and they will go crush it.

#3 – People Smarts

While IQ is certainly an important component of success, emotional IQ is perhaps more important in an industry like ours. The cleaning industry is about serving customers through unskilled labor management. If you don't have "people smarts" YOU WILL NOT SUCCEED. Here are some indicators of people smarts:

Ability to read social cues

Ability to understand and cater to the emotional needs of others even when those emotions are not clearly stated

Ability to handle conflict without alienating others

Ability to balance the needs of two parties in a way that both feel well taken care of

Ability to understand and manage one's own emotions in a variety of situations

#4 – Blue Collar Professional

Of all the attributes I'm advocating for, this is the only one unique to the building service contracting industry. Our front-line managers have a unique challenge. They must be able to relate to a low-skilled workforce one minute and then interact with managers and perhaps executives of large corporations the next. These janitorial managers must be able to train workers on cleaning toilets and pulling trash yet also be able to upsell services or negotiate contract pricing with a purchasing agent. This takes a special skill set.

A straight up white-collar manager can't relate to the blue-collar workforce, but a straight-up blue-collar worker will have difficulty dealing with corporate management. Therefore, the ideal janitorial manager is someone who possesses a professional skill set while maintaining a dash of blue-collar. Being a southerner from KY, I would refer to such a person as a professional with blue-collar roots.

Why Not Janitorial Management Experience?

In light of my article title, you may be asking yourself, why do you not view previous janitorial management experience as a key character trait of potential managers? Well, there are two primary reasons for this. First, it has been my experience that most candidates with "previous industry experience" turn out to be bad fits. They have typically been ingrained with another company's bad habits and attempt to infect my company with them. To make matters worse, they are very resistant to change. Once habits are ingrained, they are difficult to break. While about 10% of my management team has significant industry experience, the rest do not.

The second reason for my lack of excitement about janitorial management experience is that the nuts and bolts of the janitorial industry is pretty basic and can be easily trained. In fact, I would argue that we aren't in the cleaning industry as much as we are in the people management and service industry. As an industry consultant once told me, "I'd rather take a manager and teach him how to clean than take a cleaner and teach him to manage." There is much truth in that adage.

Don't Settle

Let me leave you with this little bit of encouragement. If you get the right managers and leaders on your team, your company can be a roaring success! If you settle for mediocre managers, you will have a mediocre company (and little personal freedom). So don't settle. Do the hard work of getting the right people with the qualities I listed above, then enjoy the easy work of watching them succeed!

Faith & Culture

46

Defining Success in the Cleaning Industry

Managers of cleaning companies are responsible for making sure work is done efficiently and with high quality. Leaders, on the other hand, are responsible for charting the course, clearly communicating the vision, and getting the team to voluntarily follow. Much of what gets passed off as leadership in the BSC world is nothing more than management tips and tricks. If you want to be a great leader of a great service company, you must lead from a motive greater than profit - otherwise, you are just another manager.

I have recently begun receiving coaching from a consultant who specializes in leadership development. He challenged me with a question that I want to pose to you. As a leader, this is a question you must be able to answer and communicate to your team. *"What does success look like at your business and how will you know if you have reached it?"* Don't answer too quickly, as this question is much harder than it appears at first glance.

What makes this question difficult for me is that we are programmed in today's business world to measure success solely in financial terms, i.e. profit. And even though we intuitively know this isn't the only measure of success, we rarely think through what other markers of success look like, much less find a way to measure them.

This point was driven home even more to me this morning as I was reading a book by Scott Rae titled *Business for The Common Good.* He said, "For business professionals, seeing business as something more than its moneymaking value has profound implications for how we might approach our work. If reduced to nothing more than a means to make money, it does not matter where we work or what products we make or services we offer as long as we collect an adequate paycheck."

In other words, if profit is our only or primary marker of success, then we devalue our industry, our cleaners, and our impact. Such realities should cause us to be intentional about defining success for our team in a way that aligns with our values and our view of both life and business.

So, if you want to be a true leader of your cleaning company, think long and hard about what defines success at your company and how you can know if you and your team have achieved it.

47

Devalued Workers, Reduced Profits

Henry Ford once remarked: "Why is it that I always get the whole person when what I really want is a pair of hands?" Whether many of us are willing to admit it, this is too often the prevailing attitude toward those workers who carry out the most basic of tasks at our organizations. For one of my companies, this is the janitorial team members who clean nearly 10 million square feet of facilities each night. The temptation for our leadership team and myself is to view our team members as merely robots programmed to get the job done, getting frustrated when the task is not completed exactly as instructed.

But let's face it, this frustration does us no good. In fact, treating our employees as machines only devalues them as persons, which will lower productivity and lead to decreased profits. When you hire an individual, regardless of skill or intelligence level, they have a desire to use their talents (whatever they may be) to achieve something meaningful. Viewing them as merely "a pair of hands" cuts against the grain and only makes management harder. Good leaders, on the other hand, realize the God-given desire rooted in each person and seek to connect that person with the work being done. So how can you do this?

Promote the value of the work

Our employees must see the intrinsic value of the work they are performing. They must see how their work connects with the good being brought to society. Work is voluntary giving of your time in the service of another. If you divorce an employee's work from the intrinsic value of the service provided to the end customer, you rob them of the dignity of their job. But when workers see the dignity and value of their job, productivity, performance, and retention soar. This is especially important among millennials, as studies indicate.

Give freedom within boundaries

True liberty is the ability to live freely within certain healthy restraints. The tension for employers is providing enough freedom to liberate workers to use their talents, but not so much leeway that the company is jeopardized. While this freedom/restraint tension is different for each company, it must be realized and honored. When employees don't feel like slaves, job satisfaction and performance increase.

Treat the person as a person

As unpleasant as it often may be, when you hire an individual, you get the whole person – the good, bad, and the ugly. Our tendency is to say "Business is business...keep your personal life at home." But let's be real. This is just not the way life works. When "life" happens at home, it affects the person, which affects the job. Therefore, we must set our expectation to match this reality. Treating the employee as a person and not a business machine, will gain his/her respect and trust in you as a leader. Once again, this results in increased retention, morale, and long-term productivity.

Twenty-first century companies must embrace these principles, even more so considering the growing millennial workforce. We want to pursue these goals because they are good and right in and of themselves. But secondarily, they increase morale, productivity, and profit. This is an example where putting people above profits can actually create more profit in the long run.

48

Your Business Is Inherently Religious So Get Over It

In business or professional interactions, what are the two topics you are told to avoid? You guessed it, religion and politics. In fact, the idea that religion should be confined to one's personal life is heard from nearly every corner of society. Religion is banned from schools, it's considered taboo in politics, and most think it has no place in business. Despite this being a ridiculous notion, most of us have tacitly agreed to its universal truthfulness. I'm here to tell you that in all these areas, and specifically business, nothing could be farther from the truth. Now before you write me off as a crazy, right-wing fundamentalist, please hear me out.

When I use the word religion, what I mean is one's worldview, i.e. your view of reality. A worldview is basically your fundamental beliefs about where we came from, why we are here, and how we should act (origins, purpose, and morality). These are beliefs that every person has, beliefs that we all use to make sense of life, make decisions, etc. What we believe is true about the nature of reality has a *profound* effect on how we live. Conversely, the way someone lives shows you a great deal about what they believe. Now what does this have to do with business? *Everything!*

As a business owner or leader, you are tasked with something you cannot delegate influencing the mission, values, and goals of the organization. You must communicate the "worldview" of the firm. Why does it exist? What will it accomplish? What principles will guide it? You have the sole responsibility of shaping the soul of the company. The most fundamental questions your company must ask itself are inherently religious or worldview questions.

As a business owner, God has given you a unique platform from which to declare truth to the marketplace and your team. You are not telling your team how to worship or serve God per se, something America's founders referred to as sectarian or denominational issues. Rather, you are declaring your worldview from your business platform and inviting others to participate in that mission. If your sole mission is to make money, that communicates a message that money is the sole prize of business. If you hold fast to company values such as integrity and excellence, you communicate to the world that those values are right and true and worth living for.

Now I can already hear your objections. Why not just skip the worldview/truth talk and focus on success and profit? Well, there are two reasons you can't avoid this conversation.

First, whatever you make the mission, values, and goals of your organization, that in and of itself sends a message to everyone. It tells your team and the marketplace what you value and hold as true and good. It may be hidden, but the message is sent nonetheless.

Second, human beings are inherently "religious and moral" beings. We are hard wired to know and long for what is good and true. We want to serve a greater good. We desire to live for a cause bigger than ourselves. But such a cause can only be given in light of a worldview, i.e., what is true and right about the world. And such a cause is the only thing that can unite a company to achieve something great.

Hear these words of our 1st President, George Washington, on the issue of morality and religion as it pertains to political prosperity:

> *Of all the dispositions and habits which lead to political prosperity, religion and morality are indispensable supports. In vain would that man claim the tribute of patriotism, who should labor to subvert these great pillars of human happiness, these firmest props of the duties of men and citizens...Let it simply be asked: Where is the security for property, for reputation, for life, if the sense of religious obligation desert the oaths which are the instruments of investigation in courts of justice? And let us with caution indulge the supposition that morality can be maintained without religion. Whatever may be conceded to the influence of refined education on minds of peculiar structure, reason, and experience both forbid us to expect that national morality can prevail in exclusion of religious principle.*

Prosperity, both politically and in business, spring from a right view of the world, moral virtue, and living for righteous causes. If you want a team that is engaged, passionate, excellent, and service-oriented, you must inspire them with what is right and true. Your message must resonate with them, bringing to life what is hibernating below the surface of their minds and hearts.

Don't pretend that "religion" has no place in your business. Don't attempt to create a soul-less firm. You already have a mission, values, and goals that are sending a message to your team and the marketplace. I would just challenge you to have the guts to be explicit about that message. People are starving to follow leaders with such passion. The bad reputation of "greedy big business" can only be erased by convictional leaders. Will that be you?

49

Can You Impact Your Cleaners with Company Culture?

I am completely convinced that infusing your company with a particular culture and set of values is critically important. In fact, as a business owner, this is one of your chief responsibilities, one you cannot pass off to someone else. An excellent company culture will be one of the main reasons you attract and retain the right kind of people on your team. But is it possible to infuse culture down to the cleaner level? With your cleaners spread out over many buildings, with minimal management contact, and many working only part time, can you reasonably expect to shape their attitudes and actions with the company culture?

I must admit, I have long been a skeptic of the feasibility of reaching our cleaners with our company culture of humility, integrity, excellence, and ownership mentality. Many times over the years I've vocalized that we should focus all our "culture making" effort on our management team since we have greater influence over them. But in a recent off-site strategy meeting with my sr. management team, I realized I was completely wrong.

One of the items on our agenda was company culture, and specifically how we could do a better job of infusing our team with this message. We had failed miserably in the past and we knew we could do better. But this time, instead focusing our efforts solely on the management team, we challenged the assumption that we can't reach our cleaners with the same message. Sure, we understood that our cleaners often work alone, have infrequent contact with management, and often work part time. However, we began exploring all the "touch points" we have with our cleaners, and to be quite honest, I was blown away with the opportunities we had to make an impact.

Here are some of the opportunities to reach our cleaners we discovered, broken down into four distinct stages.

Recruiting/Hiring

- Employment ads
- Application/website
- Phone screen
- In-person interview
- Employment offer

Onboarding

- Paperwork
- Orientation
- On the job training

- Uniforms and badges

On The Job

- Weekly manager interactions
- Manager phone calls/texts/emails
- Janitor's closet
- Branch picnics
- Quarterly safety "toolbox talks"

Corporate/HR

- Employee newsletter
- TEAM message at clock-in
- Birthday cards
- Employee section on website
- Video messages sent via text/email

This simple 15-minute exercise showed me, and our entire management team, that we have ample opportunities to impact our cleaners on a personal and cultural level. From recruiting all the way to exit interviews, we have more than enough "touches" to make a difference. The hurdle for us now is developing a realistic plan to make a difference at each of the four levels and then executing that plan.

Here are the actions items we came up with, broken down by stage:

- *Recruiting* – Craft interview questions that search for our values and ensure that the job offer emphasizes those traits.

- *Onboarding* – Create a company welcome video that emphasizes our culture.
- *Onboarding* – All company shirts will now have our values printed on the back.
- *On The Job* – Monthly "culture conversations" will be had with each employee by their immediate supervisor with cards to be handed out each time.
- *On The Job* – Branch picnics will be hosted at least 1x per year.
- *Corporate/HR* – A monthly video will be sent out via text/email to all employee's company-wide, created by someone in sr. leadership.

My challenge to you is this. List all the "touch points" you have with cleaners at your company, then develop 3-4 specific ways you can impact them throughout their tenure with your organization. I'm sure you will be surprised at the level of influence you can actually have. Your job is to capitalize on that opportunity for the betterment of your people, your company, and your customers.

50

One Body, Many Parts: A Theology of Cleaners

Ok, it's time for a controversial post that some of you may not agree with. But as a man led by conviction more than pragmatism, I am duty bound to share from time-to-time things many of my peers in the industry may fundamentally disagree with. And despite the modern inability to disagree with grace and respect, I am convinced that we can learn from one another even when we disagree. And while many of you will not agree with my underlying beliefs here, I am certain the practical out-workings can help you build an amazing culture at your cleaning company.

As a Christian, I am convinced of a couple of truths about reality. Human beings are made in the image of God and all work is equally valuable insofar as it serves others and the God who made them. This underlying belief creates a worldview lens through which I view my team. If I'm being honest, my personal tendency is to view myself as more important because I'm the owner. But when I'm prideful (or any of my management team) and begin to think less of my team members, a cancer is created in our organization.

In 1 Corinthians, the Apostle Paul was dealing with this situation at the church of Corinth. Some people, because of their gifts, were thinking too highly of themselves and looking down on others. This was creating some major disfunction. In this letter, he goes on to instruct the church that they are in reality one body with many parts. Just as the human body has many parts (head, neck, hands, feet, and toes), so too does the church. To lose what may seem an unimportant part of the body could in fact cause major disfunction in the body. The same is true in a church and in your company.

We must view our team, from the owner all the way down to the end cleaner, as equally important. Sure, some positions require greater responsibility and thus come with greater consequences and rewards, but intrinsically, each job is equally important. If you only think of importance in terms of the impact on net margin, you will unintentionally create a mentality that "looks down" upon the cleaner. Trust me, I know from experience that this mentality can creep in even when I'm not intentionally doing so.

But if you want a thriving culture that attracts and keeps good team members, cultivates a team willing to follow leadership, and produces a workforce that works for the good of the whole, then every person must be genuinely respected and valued. Paying lip service is not enough. It must come from the heart, which will result in actions.

So maybe you don't agree with my worldview. Fair enough. But think deeply about how you view your end cleaners and the culture you have created. Are you a servant leader or a leader of servants? Do you respect everyone, or do you expect respect because of your position? A leader worth following cares so much for his team that he lays down his own desires to respect and serve his team. In a nation accused of corporate greed, selfishness, and narcissism, we desperately need a generation of servant leaders. Why not start with the cleaning industry?

51

Eight Tips to Build a Company Culture

The longer I have been in the commercial cleaning business, the more I am convinced that a solid company culture is a key to success. The soul of your organization gives unique life to what is otherwise an ordinary service business. If you don't have a unified culture, then different parts of your company will take on different cultures. Some of those may be good and others will be toxic. As the leader of your organization, it is critical that you work toward a unified culture throughout, consisting of a vision and core values.

So how can you achieve this unified culture despite different people spread over a large geography. It is hard but let me suggest eight ways you can achieve this goal.

#1 - Establish a core purpose and values

While blatantly obvious, this step is often skipped. Get your key leader together and discover your company purpose and values. You can't push culture if you can't describe what it is.

#2 - Have weekly manager meetings

Your supervisors and managers that work with cleaners each night must be your key champions of culture. Ensure a weekly meeting with them and make culture a part of that meeting.

#3 - Record an introductory video for all new employees

With smart phones and YouTube, you can create a free video that is sent out to every new employee. This is another great way to kick start new employees.

#4 - Write a company newsletter

With Mailchimp or Microsoft Word, you can create a company newsletter and distribute it to all employees with little to no cost. This is a great way to regularly emphasize culture.

#5 - Have a periodic picnic for all employees

At my company, we have four branch offices. In the last year, they have started having local picnics for their team members. This is a great way to get everyone together, bond, and send a strong message.

#6 - Send handwritten notes to team members

Buy a stack of "Thank You" cards and make it a point to write a handwritten note to a few employees each week. If you have a large number of employees, spread this responsibility among several key leaders in the company.

#7 - Have your purpose and values listed on badges or other company items that team members see or use nightly

Putting your purpose or values in front of your team each and every night not only shows them the importance of culture, but it provides a daily reminder of it.

#8 - Reward or recognize people displaying company values.

Finally, put your money where your mouth is. Make it a point to spend some time, money, and energy in rewarding actions in line with your company culture. This sends a loud message.

52

Should We Crush Our Competition?

I grew up a sports fanatic. As a diehard Kentucky Basketball fan, my entire childhood revolved around playing basketball. I played travel ball, competed in skills tournaments, and averaged 17 points per game as a teen. In high school, I gave up basketball for my newfound love of running. After winning three team state championships and running a 4:24 mile, I went on to compete in college at a small division one school. My life revolved around competition – specifically beating that competition.

When my entrepreneurial career began in my mid-20s, I had a vision for being the biggest, best, and most dominate cleaning company in my market. Accompanying this vision was a desire to crush the competition along the way. I wanted to win. Sure, I wanted to be ethical and conduct our business with high moral standards, but my competition was just a roadblock to reaching my ultimate goal.

But in the last few years, I've been forced to rethink this mindset. Through the relationships I've made in the BSCAI and our Elite BSC Mastermind Group, I have come to view my competition as friends. In fact, I want to see them succeed because I care about them, their people, their families, and the industry. And as for the rest of the competition that I don't know, I'm sure I would want the same for them if I had the chance to get to know them.

So where does this leave me (and you) now? First, we can't in good conscience want our competition to fail, nor can we seek to undermine their success. Second, short of undermining your own company, we should help our friends in the industry (even our direct competitors). Socialists believe in a fixed pie that results in "haves" and "have nots." But I reject this notion. If people are creating as God designed them, the pie is always growing and those who serve well will have plenty of business.

The problem with focusing too heavily on market share or competition is that it cultivates selfishness in our organization, undermining the very foundation of our industry, serving others. The solution to our competition focus is customer focus. Striving for the best possible service at a responsible price will inevitably result in a successful company (all other things being equal). So don't seek to crush the competition. Hit home runs in service and relationships with your customers and your team. Competition will soon fade in importance and friendships will take its place. Give it a try!

Made in the USA
Columbia, SC
23 December 2022

74923283R00130